OUT OF THE OFFICE

A THEOLOGY OF MINISTRY

Conversations in Minstry, Volume 3

ROBERT D. CORNWALL

Energion Publications
Gonzalez, FL
2017

ISBN10: 1-63199-373-9
ISBN13: 978-1-63199-373-2
Library of Congress Control Number: 2017938739

Energion Publications
P. O. Box 841
Gonzalez, FL 32560

energion.com
pubs@energion.com

TABLE OF CONTENTS

SERIES PREFACE

Parish ministry can be an exciting and challenging vocation. This has always been the case, but it is perhaps even truer today. At least in the European and North American contexts, institutional forms of religion are finding themselves pushed to the sidelines. Their purpose and value has been questioned, and with these questions come further questions about the professional status of those who are called to serve these congregations. A generation ago, congregational ministers might see themselves as members of a professional class, like that of medical doctors and attorneys. The Academy of Parish Clergy, the sponsor of this book series, was founded with just that vision—to encourage and enhance the professional practice of parish ministry. This was to be accomplished by setting professional standards, including the encouragement to engage in regular continuing education, and then providing a means of accountability to those standards. Although the broader culture has raised questions about the professional standing of parish clergy, the need for professional standards, continuing education, and accountability remains as important today as ever before. This is because the world in which ministry is being done is ever changing, and therefore clergy must adapt, learn new skills, and reposition themselves for a new day. It is helpful, therefore, to walk in the company of others who are also engaged in similar kinds of ministry.

What makes parish ministry both exciting and challenging is that most clergy are generalists. They're like the family practitioner, dealing with a wide variety of issues and people. No day is exactly the same, for they serve as teachers, preachers, worship leaders, providers of pastoral care, administrators, and social justice leaders. They may be more gifted in some areas than others, but ultimately, they find themselves engaged in a wide variety of tasks that often push them to the limits of ability and endurance. It is not a vocation that can be undertaken on one's own, and for a variety of reasons parish ministers need to find a community of others who share this calling, so that they might find encouragement, support, and ideas for dealing with parish life and ministry in the broader world.

Part of the founding vision of the Academy of Parish Clergy was to facilitate this need to find a community of peers, and with this in mind, Academy members were encouraged to create and join in Colleague Groups, where they could encourage one another and explore issues that confront clergy in their daily ministry, often using the "Case Study Method," which was emerging at the time among the professions. That model is still available, but it is the hope of the editors of this series that these books will also provide a foundation for conversation in clergy groups.

This vision continues to sustain the Academy more than forty years after its founding, and the APC book series, *Conversations in Ministry*, seeks to extend this vision by offering to clergy, books written primarily by practicing clergy for practicing clergy dealing with the issues that confront them in ministry today. Each book, published in partnership with Energion Publications, will be brief and focused (under 100 pages). Each book is designed to encourage reflection and conversation among clergy. The editors and authors of these books hope that the books will be taken up by groups of clergy and inspire conversation.

It is important to point out the use of the preposition "in." The conversations that are envisioned here are not simply about ministry, but are designed to emerge from within the context of ministry. Although the initial book covers a variety of issues facing clergy, future books will focus on specific issues including clergy ethics, self-care, preaching, worship leadership, congregational administration, use of social media. Each book will include discussion questions that can aid group conversation, but also individual reflection. Each book will reflect the purpose of the series, but each author will take the conversation in the direction the topic suggests. May this series of books be a blessing to all who read them.

Robert D. Cornwall, APC
General Editor

ORIENTATION

Ministry is something clergy do—most often within the confines of a church building or at least among the members of a congregation. It can involve preaching, teaching, celebrating the sacraments, and providing pastoral care. But is this all that the word conveys? Since the series of books in which this appears is designed to create a conversation among clergy on matters related to parish ministry, a discussion of a theology of ministry would invite a theological reflection on what clergy do in a parish context. Such is the case here, except that I would like to broaden the concept of the parish to include the local congregation as well as the broader world in which a congregation exists. This isn't an either/or proposition. It's a both/and. Nonetheless, I take as a starting point the premise of John Wesley that the world is our parish. Therefore, I'm assuming that the context in which the readers of this book do ministry will include the congregation and will extend to the neighborhood and beyond.

I write this book with the Academy of Parish Clergy in mind. As I do so I am conscious of the fact that while the Academy has been a predominantly Christian organization, it has a broader vision of being a gathering of clergy from across the religious spectrum. Keeping in mind this more inclusive vision, theologies of ministry are rooted in specific faith communities. I have long been active in interfaith work, but my own theology of ministry and my calling to ministry is distinctly Christian. Therefore, this book reflects my context as a Christian pastor, writing to other Christian clergy, inviting them to reflect on their own theologies of ministry. At the same time, I hope that my reflections might encourage persons who do not share my theological context to look to their own traditions for theological resources that would guide their own ministries in the world.

If our theological reflection on ministry is rooted in the Christian tradition, and therefore, is rooted in the witness of scripture, then we need to ask ourselves whether ministry is something to which the whole people of God are called, or whether the call is limited to those who are ordained. While I expect that most readers of this book will be clergy or those preparing for such ministry, this is an important question to keep in mind. As I read scripture, it seems that ministry is both a shared vocation that includes the whole people of God, and a calling to which some are called for purposes of leadership and equipping of the saints. So, we could say that among the whole people of God who are called to ministry, some are called to a vocation that is called the clergy. While the gifts of the Spirit are poured out upon all, among those gifts are gifts of leadership and teaching.[1]

While I believe that ministry is something shared within the community of faith, the focus of this book series is conversation among those called to vocational or professional ministry. The idea that ministry is a profession among professions (like medicine, law, business), can obscure the sense of divine call. It is rather easy for those of us who are engaged in this work to become pragmatic and mechanical in our ministrations. We can become dependent solely on our training and certification to sustain our work. Since many of us derive our livelihood from doing these things well—or at least good enough to please those who have the authority to hire, fire, or reassign us—the focus can be on doing the job well as measured by more secular metrics. Those metrics focus on satisfying the customer.

While professional standards of behavior and training are important (upon being ordained many of us will be required to sign off on some form of ministry ethics—the Academy of Parish Clergy has its own ethical statement members are to affirm), professional standards are not enough. There is need for us to understand ministry from a theological point of view. While many of us took

---

1   I flesh this out in my book *Unfettered Spirit: Spiritual Gifts for the New Great Awakening*, (Gonzalez, FL: Energion Publications, 2013).

a theology of ministry class in seminary, how often do we look at our work through a theological lens? Could it be that engaging in theological reflection on one's ministry throughout the course of one's ministry might help sustain a sense of call for the long term?

My hope is that this book can serve as an invitation to engage in ongoing theological reflection on the work of ministry. I write for clergy as a member of the clergy. I share the call to vocational ministry, but my own understanding of ministry is rooted in a theology of spiritual gifts that embraces all God's people. As we engage theologically our own calling and our own work it is important to keep this in focus.

In the course of the conversation, we will move from the question of the nature of our theology (for our theologies will differ depending on our tradition) onward through conversations about definitions of ministry, giftedness, missional context, ministry context, ministry practices, and ordination. I realize that some who read this book will have been engaging in ordained ministry for decades, and some of what appears here might be old hat. Nonetheless, I believe that it doesn't matter how long we've been on this journey, it's good to stop and do some theological reflection. It's easy to forget those foundations. I'm also hoping that some who read this book are in the first stages of preparation. Hopefully, this invitation to theological reflection will help such persons put down a theological anchor for their journey forward into ordained ministry. This is important, in my view, because the journey ahead will not always be easy. Each chapter below includes an action/reflection component and questions for discussion. Whether the book is read as part of a group discussion or by individuals, the hope is that one's sense of ministry will be broadened through theological reflection.

CHAPTER 1

WHAT IS MY THEOLOGY?

If we're going to do theological reflection on vocational ministry, it would be wise to define our terms. That is, what is theology and what tools/resources should we avail ourselves of if we're to do theology? If you are already ordained, perhaps you were asked these kinds of questions prior to your ordination for parish ministry. This is more than an academic question, because those called to parish ministry are, by calling, theologians. In fact, those called to parish ministry serve as both pastoral theologians and as public theologians.

Theology is more than an academic exercise that we engage in during seminary and then leave behind when we go to work in a congregation. This is because our belief systems and our practices of ministry are intertwined. Not only is this true, but we should expect that our theologies will evolve and mature over time. New experiences in ministry will require engaging our belief systems in new ways. For instance, debates/discussions about marriage equality often turn on one's life experiences. Relationships may call for rethinking previous understandings, or at least challenge them. This should lead to a new engagement with one's theology.

Since theology is, at its base, thinking about God [Greek *theos* (God) + *logos* (word/thinking)], every person of faith does theology at some level. When I do theology, I do so from a distinctly Christian perspective, though my theology is influenced by conversation with an increasingly diverse set of conversation partners, whether they be academic theologians or members of my congregation, fellow clergy or strangers on a bench. While there is a place for the specialist, theology is not a work that should be left solely to specialists. Clergy are, by training (one would hope) and position, theological generalists who are called to help congregations engage in theological work.[1]

As we move through this conversation it is important to recognize that those called to vocational ministry are first and foremost congregation-based theological teachers. They are called to equip the people of God to engage in serious theological conversation. Pastor/theologian Dr. Bruce Epperly writes of the importance of theological education in the congregation, encouraging clergy to take up their calling to encourage theological exploration among the laity in the congregation.

> In a time in which many assert that post-modernism privileges experience over doctrine, open-ended theological reflection has become more essential in the pulpit and the congregational classroom. Congregants need to nurture the mind as well as the spirit and heart to creatively face the challenges of our pluralistic age. They need safe places in which to explore their faith questions and challenge childhood ideas about God and humankind.[2]

Theologian Joe Jones challenges those clergy who do not think it important to continue growing theologically, suggesting that "it is a self-contradiction to claim to be a pastor of a Christian congregation and to admit that one is either ignorant of or simply uninterested in the theological language of the church concerning the reality of God and the life, death, and resurrection of Jesus of Nazareth."[3]

Doing theological work in the congregation helps those who are part of the community define their identity as being Christian. Even non-creedal traditions, like my own, have a theological iden-

1   Philip Clayton with Tripp Fuller, *Transforming Christian Theology for Church and Society,* (Minneapolis: Fortress Press, 2010), pp. 2-3.
2   Bruce Epperly, "Encouraging Lay Theology," *Alban at Duke Divinity School,* (https://alban.org/2016/08/16/bruce-epperly-encouraging-lay-theology).
3   Joe R. Jones, *A Lover's Quarrel: A Theologian and His Beloved Church,* (Eugene, OR: Cascade Books, 2014), p. 198.

tity. They believe certain things, even if they do not use these beliefs as authoritative tests of fellowship. The question for clergy is how to create space for intelligent inquiry in matters of great spiritual and ethical importance.

When we talk about theology and doctrine and dogma the word "believe" will come up in the conversation. The term has faced significant critique of late, especially within the kinds of mainline Protestant circles I frequent. There is increasing discomfort with narrow definitions of theology. The suggestion made by many, including clergy, is that orthopraxis (right action) is of greater importance than orthodoxy (right belief). The truth seems to me to be that the two are connected. What I believe about God influences my practice, even as my practice informs my theologizing.

Even if we conclude that to believe is not the same thing as assenting to doctrinal statements, which are themselves human attempts to work out the significance of beliefs at an intellectual level and should not be absolutized, I'm assuming we all have beliefs. That is, we all have a theology, whether it corresponds to an official statement. Otherwise, faith communities simply become service organizations. There's nothing wrong with service organizations, but they're very different entities. Unfortunately, congregations can become little more than service organizations if they do not root themselves in the divine. That means, for Christians at least, actions are rooted in worship. The second commandment, to love one's neighbor, follows upon the first commandment, which is to love God. As Christian psychologist Richard Beck puts it, "according to the One Love view, loving our neighbors is the *complete and full expression* of what it means to love God. In the words of Romans 13:10, 'Love does no harm to a neighbor. Therefore, love is the fulfillment of the law.'"[1]

Belief involves putting trust in someone or something, but if we are going to put our trust in someone then there must be something of substance there to trust. This is where theology comes into

---

1   Richard Beck, *Reviving Old Scratch: Demons and the Devil for Doubters and the Disenchanted,* (Minneapolis: Fortress Press, 2016), p. 90.

play. One possible way of engaging one's theological vision is to write out one's own personal credo. If I am a Christian, for instance, what do I believe about God, Jesus, the church, salvation? In other words, we seek to answer the question that Jesus put to his disciples: "Who do you say that I am? (Matthew 16:15).[1]

THINKING THEOLOGICALLY ABOUT MINISTRY

As we work out our own theology, we who are called to parish ministry will need to engage in theological reflection on the work we do. So, for instance, if we define ministry as service [*diakonia*] to God and to God's people, we'll need to ask how God fits into our understanding of that service. As I noted earlier, in my understanding of ministry all members of the community are engaged in the work of ministry, therefore, we will need to consider how these various ministries reflect our vision of God.

The discipline of doing theology involves more than our thoughts about God. If we embrace a Trinitarian vision of God, as do I, then theology will also include reflections that are rooted in Christology and Pneumatology. And if, as Paul suggests, the church is the body of Christ, then Christology (and pneumatology) lead us to the question of ecclesiology—consideration of the nature of the church.

If we begin with the first order question—in the context of parish ministry, how does my view of God get reflected in my sense of call? If we envision God as distant overlord does this vision get reflected in an aloof and hierarchical form of ministry? If we think of God as standing near at hand, then does our sense of call take on a more intimate form of ministry? Do ideas about divine wrath and divine love contribute to the way in which we envision ministry and practice it?

Moving on to Christology, when we read the gospels or consider the testimony of the letters of the New Testament, who do

---

1   Clayton's book *Transforming Christian Theology* provides an excellent introduction to the kind of initial theological work that can benefit our own theological reflection on the call to ministry.

we meet there? Do we not find one who is teacher, preacher, leader of prayer, healer, reconciler, and prophet? If I may, I would like to add in the category of community organizer. Our Christological understandings of ministry also flows from the way in which Jesus is understood to be the incarnation of God in the world, how he humbled himself and took on the form of a servant, even though he was in the form of God (Philippians 2:1-11). Then, in 2 Corinthians 5 Paul speaks of God reconciling the world to God's self through Christ, and then giving to us the ministry of reconciliation. This is a Christological concept—so how does this calling get reflected in one's ministry? We can ask a further Christological question—how do those called to vocational ministry continue the ministry that Jesus began in his own lifetime? We see this expressed in the call of the Apostles from among the disciples, to a ministry of leadership with the community, a ministry that includes teaching, preaching, and healing.[1]

Turning to Pneumatology (the doctrine of the Holy Spirit), how do we understand giftedness and empowerment? Kathleen Cahalan writes: "the Spirit constitutes the church through gifts of discipleship and vocation, including ministry . . . When we discern gifts for ministry, we are looking for these people and gifts related to these practices."[2] When the church looks to call out those who would fill these ministerial responsibilities that have been discerned from Jesus' own ministry, the church looks for those with the appropriate charisms or gifts. Pneumatology also allows us to broaden our ministry horizons. The Spirit embraces difference. The Spirit fell on Cornelius and his household opening up Peter's understanding of the household of God (Acts 10-11).

Ministry occurs within the context of the church, but what is the church in theological terms, and how does this influence the

---

1 Kathleen Cahalan, *Introducing the Practice of Ministry*, (Collegeville, MN: Liturgical Press, 2010), p. 59.
2 Cahalan, *Introducing the Practice of Ministry*, loc. 1280-1281 Kindle edition. See also Robert D. Cornwall, *Unfettered Spirit: Spiritual Gifts for a New Great Awakening*, (Gonzalez, FL: Energion Publications, 2013).

way we envision ministry? We tend to think of church in institutional terms, but in this context, we need to move beyond this
rather narrow category, and think of church theologically as body
of Christ and as community. Community, as Bonhoeffer reminds
us, "is not an ideal we have to realize, but rather a reality created
by God in Christ in which we may participate." He goes on to
write that "the more clearly we learn to recognize that the ground
and strength and promise of all our community is in Jesus Christ
alone, the more calmly we will learn to think about our community
and pray and hope for it."[1] He writes this in response to those who
bring to the community expectations and demands that destroy
rather than create true Christian community. When we conceive
of the church as body of Christ and community, rather than as
simply an institution (though it is true that there is an institutional
dimension to the church) we can better understand what it means
for ministry to be an ecclesial activity. As Kathleen Cahalan notes,
ministry is ecclesial not because those called out are the "'head of
the church'; but because their gifts of leadership are recognized,
called forth and 'ordained by the community.'"[2] I should note that
for practical reasons Cahalan distinguishes between discipleship
and ministry. Ministry emerges out of discipleship, and among
disciples some are ordained for leadership.

Cahalan's orientation is Roman Catholic, so that colors her
perspective to a degree, but the point is important—there are theological foundations that enable us to see ministry as more than
function. The way in which ministry exists will evolve over time
as Christians engage culture and era, but there is still a touchstone
upon which we discern a pathway in the present moment. What we
are learning, or I hope we are learning, is that a call to leadership
(ordination) does not make someone a special kind of Christian,
but simply designates a form of ministry that reflects the nature

---

1   Dietrich Bonhoeffer, *Life Together. Prayer book of the Bible* (Dietrich
    Bonhoeffer Works), Geffrey B. Kelly, ed.; Daniel W. Bloesch and James H.
    Burtness, trans., (Minneapolis: Fortress Press, 1996), 5:38.
2   Cahalan, *Introducing the Practice of Ministry*, p. 59

and purpose of God (and I hesitate to use the word "purpose" lest I be seen as reflecting a more deterministic view of faith).

Sources for Doing Theology

Theological reflection on the call to ministry will need resources that engender conversation. For Christians, the starting place will be Scripture, which is the most ancient and authoritative source of reflection on the things of God. For Protestants, who often speak of the principle of *sola scriptura*, the text of Scripture provides essential guidance. But even if we give it primacy, Scripture is not the only source that we turn to in our theological work. One of the most common expressions of a broader scope of theological sources is known as the *Wesleyan Quadrilateral*: Scripture, tradition, reason, experience. It should be noted that these are not considered four equal sources of authority. Rather, when engaging Scripture, which holds primacy as the church's sacred text, we make use of tradition, reason, and experience as critical tools for interpreting the normative source, which is Scripture.

For many Jews and Christians, Scripture (in whatever form is accepted as authoritative) is normative, while for others it is at least the touchstone, the starting point for doing theological reflection. It is, however, not the end. The issue, as Philip Clayton notes in his book *Transforming Theology*, is not whether you get your doctrine of Scripture correct, but whether you can "deeply, intelligently, and constantly," use it to look at the big issues of life—including the nature of Christian ministry.[1]

As we work with Scripture, if we're discerning people, we will quickly discover that there is a deep and wide chasm separating us from the time and place where these texts emerged. Tradition helps us build the necessary bridge between then and now, by bringing to mind the teachings and experiences of those who have lived the faith across time. This wisdom helps counteract our own presuppositions and opinions. The function of tradition isn't to provide

---

1   Clayton, *Transforming Christian Theology*, p. 25.

infallible facts. It is, instead, "the resource of many generations and many centuries of readers who have struggled with what God could be saying in and through the scriptural reports on the Hebrew tradition, on Jesus' life, and on the early church."[1] This is an important corrective to the hubris of my own tradition, which thought it could jump back over the centuries and restore New Testament Christianity. What emerged was a very modern, nineteenth century, American version of the Christian faith.[2]

Then comes *experience*. We like to turn to it because it seems personal and relevant, but that's not the only reason to engage our life experience. Experience can often push us to reflect more deeply on the things of the spirit. Experience is also important because it is difficult to believe something that conflicts with our experience. The challenge of experience is that living as we do in a privatistic and individualistic world, we can make our experience normative. That can be dangerous for us and for our neighbors. Experience therefore is often a good starting point for doing theological reflection and it's a good check on our belief systems.

Finally, we must acknowledge the importance of *reason*, which interestingly enough—considering that we are the products of an age of reason—seems to be underutilized. In matters of faith, we often pay little heed to science, except perhaps the recent interest in psychology. We find it difficult to wrestle deeply with our experience and our inherited traditions, but reason allows us to bring experience and tradition into deeper conversation with Scripture. Theologians have often turned to philosophy to provide terminology and criteria for doing theology. One needn't be an academic to do this kind of work, but one must be willing to engage one's faith with the mind. As we have this conversation we gain a better understanding of the world around us and what it means to live in

1   Clayton, *Transforming Christian Theology*, p. 25.
2   The tradition I speak of is the Stone-Campbell Movement, of which my branch is known as the Christian Church (Disciples of Christ). I have written about these issues in *Freedom in Covenant: Reflections on the Distinctive Values and Practices of the Christian Church (Disciples of Christ)*, (Eugene, OR: Wipf and Stock, 2015).

this context. While there may be other sources, these four are the most recognized, and thus foundational to providing us with the resources to look at ministry theologically.

ACTION AND REFLECTION:

Sit down in a quiet place and write out a personal statement of faith. Take into consideration the four resources for doing theology. Ask yourself whether your statement of faith has changed over time or stayed the same. If your theological understandings have stayed the same over time why do you think this is true? If it has changed, why has it changed?

Questions for Discussion:

1. What is Theology? How does your definition of theology impact the way you look at ministry?

2. If clergy, do you see yourself as a theologian (a generalist/ pastoral theologian, but still a theologian)?

3. What is your response to theologian Joe Jones' statement that it is a "self-contradiction to claim to be a pastor of a Christian congregation and to admit that one is either ignorant of or simply uninterested in the theological language of the church concerning the reality of God and the life, death, and resurrection of Jesus of Nazareth?"

4. What are the theological resources that you most look to and why? How do these resources enhance your vision of ministry?

CHAPTER 2

WHAT IS MINISTRY?

The task before us is to develop a theology of ministry. We've discussed the importance of doing theology and some of the key resources that are used to do this work, which for some readers this may be old hat, but it is good to have a refresher periodically. With this under our belt we move on to defining the meaning and purpose of ministry. We need to consider whether ministry is a special vocation to which a select few are called through the process and ritual of ordination, or whether it is something that all adherents have a share in? Martin Luther spoke of the "priesthood of all believers," an idea that has biblical roots, but he didn't reject the idea of a special class of ordained leadership—though he rejected the idea that ordination was a sacrament. There are those, especially in the Anabaptist tradition, who embrace a flatter sense of church and ministry. Some faith communities take a rather anti-clerical attitude toward the idea of a special ordained status. Although I believe that ministry is a shared vocation, and that all ministry is rooted in our spiritual gifts, I see the importance of acknowledging the importance of a ministry of leadership and teaching for the community—especially theological leadership (the gift of teacher and pastor). But from whence does this call emerge?

Ministry is often understood in relationship to the tasks of—leadership, teaching, preaching, pastoral care, worship leadership, and administration. Those who engage in these tasks are the ministers. These duly authorized persons engage in work on behalf of the community that they serve. Kathleen Cahalan suggests that ministry is constituted by a "gift received through faith and baptism, charism, and vocation that is acknowledged by the community in rituals of commissioning, installation, and ordination; and as a practice that exists within a diverse array of ecclesial contexts, roles and relationships."[1] The question then is: how do these charisms relate to the charisms of those not called by the church to ordained ministry?

Although each faith community or denominational tradition has its own definition of ministry, recent attempts to reach an ecumenical consensus could be instructive to our conversation. Consider the definition of ministry developed by the Faith and Order Commission (World Council of Churches), which was published as part of the *Baptism, Eucharist and Ministry Document* (1982). This document suggests that while all are called to ministry, there is precedent in the ministry of Jesus for recognizing certain persons for specific forms of ministry, ministry that is recognized by the church through ordination, persons authorized for leadership in the church.

> 15. The authority of the ordained minister is rooted in Jesus Christ, who has received it from the Father (Matthew 28:18), and who confers it by the Holy Spirit through the act of ordination. This act takes place within a community which accords public recognition to a particular person. Because Jesus came as one who serves (Mark 10:45; Luke 22:27), to be set apart means to be consecrated to service. Since ordination is essentially a setting apart with prayer for the gift of the Holy Spirit, the authority of the ordained ministry is not to be understood as the possession of the ordained person but as a gift for the continuing edification of the body in and for which the minister has been ordained. Authority has the character of responsibility before God and is exercised with the cooperation of the whole community.[2]

---

1   Cahalan, *Introducing the Practice of Ministry,* p. 55.
2   *Baptism, Eucharist, and Ministry Document*; Faith and Order Paper number 111. http://www.oikoumene.org/en/resources/documents/commissions/faith-and-order/i-unity-the-church-and-its-mission/baptism-eucharist-and-ministry-faith-and-order-paper-no-111-the-lima-text/@@download/file/FO1982_111_en.pdf. (Last accessed, April 1, 2017).

This definition of ministry offers several points of departure. First, this definition offers a clear connection to the Trinity. The authority given to the one who is ordained comes from God the Father to the Son who passes it on to the ordained by the Holy Spirit. This definition, even if not explicitly sacramental in nature, has a sacramental flavor to it. It also lends itself well to a hierarchical vision of ministry. The definition also assumes that this ministry takes place within the community that gives public recognition to the call. As such the authority of one engaging in ministry is not something one accords to oneself. Because this call to service comes as divine gift, it is not a personal possession that can be earned or owned, it is simply expressed through acts of leadership that edify the body of Christ. By implication this definition rules out Lone Ranger forms of ministry.

As we contemplate this definition, we might ask how it relates to the ministry of the rest of the *laos*. That is, to what degree are the ministries of those the church ordains related to the laity, for both clergy and laity are part of the *laos* (people) of God?

ORDERED MINISTRY IN A FLAT CHURCH?

The definition of ministerial authority found in the *Baptism, Eucharist and Ministry Document* has hierarchical assumptions. It is a vision that has tradition behind it and is the product of significant theological conversation across a broad spectrum of the church. It is, however, not the only vision available to us. We've already noted that most Christian traditions, at least in theory, affirm the priesthood of all believers. One can hold to such a view along with a more formal hierarchical view (all are priests, but not all are leaders of priests), but there are others who would do away with titles and even forms of ordination. In contrast to what they would deem a hierarchical model of ministry, they offer a flat model.

One of the more outspoken advocates of a flat church model of church leadership is Tony Jones. Jones advocates for what he calls a "relational ecclesiology." It too is rooted in the doctrine of the Trinity, but Jones looks to Jürgen Moltmann's vision of the social

Trinity for inspiration. In this model, the church is a community that reflects the community of persons within the Trinity. Using Moltmann as fodder for his thinking, Jones envisions a world in which the sacred/secular divide has been eliminated. Thus, the church is not a sacred space, but exists fully within the world itself. The church is not a sanctuary with clergy who mediate the sacred. It's important to note that at least in Jones' estimation, and as practiced at the church he participates with, no one person is credentialed or authorized to consecrate/officiate at the Eucharist. Anyone in the community can be tapped to share in leadership at the Table. It is important to note that Jones embraces a rather radical form of congregationalism that eschews entanglements with denominational bureaucracies. In contrast to the traditional idea of the pastor as overseer, he suggests that we look for guidance in Moltmann's vision of the Christological office of "friend." By focusing on this office churches can become egalitarian fellowships. As to how this affects those who are clergy, he writes:

These congregations have largely abdicated the traditional titles taken by clergy (Reverend, Pastor, Father), titles which sometimes serve to prop up traditional hierarchical structures and the attitudes of domination and submission that so often accompany them. Now, at a time when public distrust of clergy is on the rise due to the many public scandals of the past several decades, clergypersons may do well to relinquish antiquated and honorific titles in favor of a single designator, like "friend," that clearly communicates an equivalency between all members of a faith community.[1]

So, what would ministry look like if we were to embrace this concept of church? Is it feasible?

I should note that most of the emergent-style churches I know of often view themselves as expressions of this kind of flat ecclesiology, but at the same time are led by charismatic-type leaders. Whether they have credentials (and I believe most have them), they have the kind of personalities that draws people to them. So, where does this authority derive from? They might say that it comes from

---

1   Tony Jones, *The Church is Flat*, (Minneapolis: JoPa Productions, 2011), p. 172.

God, but what is the confirmation of that sense of call? These are questions that we need to consider as we look at the way in which people are called to do ministry in this new and oft changing world.

At what point does a person become a minister? Answers to this question will be influenced by the definition of ministry. In a flat vision of ministry, the moment one becomes a minister is at baptism. Thus, all baptized Christians, at least in theory if not practice, are ministers. On the other hand, the title of minister might be reserved for those called by the church to lead and equip those who are called to be disciples, and this calling might be affirmed through ordination or laying on of hands? I find intriguing the suggestion made by Kathleen Cahalan, a Roman Catholic, that we should distinguish between discipleship and ministry. In her vision ministry is "the vocation of leading disciples in the life of discipleship for the sake of God's mission in the world."[1]

However, one defines ministry, and however one determines when one becomes a minister, there is, in the New Testament the provision for distinctive forms of leadership for the good of the community.

NEW TESTAMENT AND CHRISTIAN LEADERSHIP

It should be noted up front that when we talk about New Testament forms of Christian leadership and authority, we're not talking about simply one prescribed format. Although many have tried to find the one pattern, there are many patterns that seem to be location specific. There are, however, clear signs that the early church didn't lack for structure. Although having different names and functions, there were officers and leaders in each community. These various models provide the foundation for developing understandings of ministry in the contemporary church.

In many ways, the churches at Corinth and Ephesus offer contrasting examples of ecclesial structures. The Corinthian church appears to have had an informal structure, one guided by spiritually discerning elders (therefore it is not surprising that we find the bulk

---

1   Cahalan, *Introducing the Practice of Ministry*, p. 50.

of teaching on spiritual gifts in a letter written to this church). But, remember that this is written by Paul early in the life of the Christian movement. It also should be noted too this church seems to have a lot of difficulty ordering itself. Ephesus, on the other hand, seems to have had a more formal structure that included apostles, prophets, evangelists, pastors and teachers (Ephesians 4:11). This letter, possibly written sometime after Paul's death, suggests that over time churches may have discerned the need for more structure. Finally, there is the first letter to Timothy, written, it seems, to the pastor of the Ephesian church by a later disciple of Paul (later first century), where you have bishops (elders), presbyters, and deacons. In its discussion of presbyters (elders/pastors) and *episcope* (bishops/ elders), the Pastorals flesh out a relationship between the church and its leaders that looks much different from the much earlier Corinthian church. By the beginning of the second century the church had moved into even more formal forms of leadership, as can be seen in the writings of early leaders such as Ignatius of Antioch.

Even if we accept the premise that the Pastoral Letters are relatively late, and not from the hand of Paul, the descriptions found there of elders (*episkopos*), deacons, and widows merit some attention as these terms continue to be in use in our churches, even though they are used differently from tradition to tradition. For instance, elder and deacon are two different orders of ordained ministry within the United Methodist Church, while they are lay offices in the Disciples of Christ.

The focus of the Pastoral Letters is on the personal and moral qualifications for ministry, not the educational ones. Elders should be able to teach and manage their own finances, so that they can manage the finances of the church. It appears that the author of this letter assumes that the congregation will have a plurality of elders, not just one (1 Timothy 3:1; Titus 1:5-7). Therefore, the author is not envisioning the monarchical episcopate that emerged early in the second century. While some would distinguish between those with the ministry of oversight (*episkopos*) and that of eldership (*presbuteros*) they seem to be used interchangeably. There is, interestingly enough, encouragement to provide financial support for those called to this role, possibly so they can devote more time to the church's ministry than would be allowed if they had to earn their entire way outside the church (1 Timothy 5:17, 19).

The second office mentioned in the Pastorals was that of deacon (1 Timothy 3:8-13). The Greek word is *diakonos*, which can be translated as minister or servant. Paul describes himself as a *diakonos* (Colossians 1:17, 23, 25) and he calls Phoebe a *diakonos* as well (Romans 16:1). If this was an office in the Pauline churches, then Paul was willing to accept the title as would Phoebe, suggesting that women were included in this ministry. Again, the emphasis is on personal qualifications rather than on particular responsibilities. It is possible that they were entrusted with overseeing the church's work of social service, or perhaps they oversaw the financial side of church life. Reference is often made to Acts 6, where seven persons are set aside to provide service to the widows of the Hellenists. In creating this office, the Apostles sought to protect their time so they could devote their attention to teaching (Acts 6:1-7). No connection is made in the Pastorals, however, to this story.

In 1 Timothy 5:3-16 we find an order of widows described. Instructions are given as to who should be enrolled and how they should act. A widow was to be older than sixty, married only once, have a reputation for good works, had raised children, shown hospitality to strangers, washed the feet of strangers, and assisted those in distress. The nature of their assignments is not defined, but reference to this order is intriguing. There does not seem to be much difference between this role and that of the *diaconate*. What is clear is these widows, now alone in the world, were to be supported by the church, and at the very least they were to engage in a ministry of intercession.

Whether any of these offices, from elder to widow, relate to contemporary ministerial offices, can't be fully discerned. We can, however, find valuable lessons in the word of advice given by the author of 1 Timothy to a younger colleague. The older, more experienced, pastor encourages the younger pastor not let the people despise his youth. Instead, Timothy's mentor tells him to set an example in his speech and conduct, and "give attention to the public reading of Scripture, to exhorting, to teaching." Finally, Timothy is told not to "neglect the gift that is in you, which was given to you through prophecy with the laying on of hands by the council of elders" (1 Timothy 4:12-14). This reference to a gift given by laying on of hands is the biblical foundation for an ordained ministry. Later in the letter, the author tells Timothy to rekindle this gift. Vocational ministry, therefore, is in the words of this biblical writer a matter of giftedness, which must be rekindled on occasion.[1]

If ministry is rooted in giftedness, is there a place for a more "priestly" form of leadership? By priests, I mean those who are set aside to intercede on behalf of the people of God. In most mainline Protestant traditions (the Disciples of Christ seeming to be something of an anomaly) there is a category of ministry called "minister of word and sacrament." Such ministries have liturgical/sacramental functions reserved to them. One could say that ministers of the sacrament perform a priestly role, especially if clergy are required to properly perform sacramental duties, such as consecrate the Eucharist or baptize. As a counterpoint to such a view we could consider the somewhat anomalous practice of the Christian Church (Disciples of Christ), in which lay elders may preach and celebrate the sacraments without being ordained to ministry (though some Disciples churches ordain elders). Even in most Disciples churches, however, clergy preside at the Table (Elders pray over the elements, while the pastor will recite the words of institution) and perform baptisms. But if there is a priesthood of all believers to which one is ordained through baptism, should there be a separate order of priestly ministers? This is a question that each tradition should wrestle with, though I'm not sure that a strict distinction can be made, at least on biblical grounds.

As it has come down through the centuries, ordination is a process that sets men and women apart for specific forms of vocational

---

1   Donald Messer, *Contemporary Images of Christian Ministry,* (Nashville: Abingdon Press, 1989), 64.

ministry. Congregations, denominations, seminaries are charged with discerning whether candidates have the gifts and calling for this type of ministry. Following the instructions of 1 Timothy, the church (whatever its appropriate form in each tradition) lays hands on the candidate, commissioning that person and praying that the Spirit might indwell and empower them for service to the church and the world (1 Timothy 4:14).[1] Whatever authority such a person has within the congregation is rooted in that congregation. It is the Spirit who gifts, empowers, and commissions, and thus bishops, elders, congregations simply are the conveyers of that tradition. By recognizing a pastor's ordination, a congregation receives that person's leadership and guidance. Tradition and history help us understand how this authority should be exercised in the life of a congregation. Though our churches may use a variety of structural forms, it is important to recognize that the church is not a democracy, ruled by majority vote. It is also not an autocracy, the rule of an elite group of clergy, or a monarchy for that matter. The church is guided and led by the Spirit of God who speaks through pastors, elders, deacons, prophets, and just ordinary believers.

MINISTRY AS PROFESSION

Is vocational ministry to be understood as a profession? In many ways, vocational ministry—at least in mainline Protestant churches—has the marks of professionalism. There are certain educational standards that need to be met. There are credentialing bodies that grant ordination and standing. Most mainline Protestant denominations have ethical standards that clergy are expected to embrace. Clergy, for instance, are expected to keep in confidence what they are told in counseling sessions. These bodies might require clergy to participate in continuing education if standing is to be continued. This is a rather modern expectation. It certainly doesn't have biblical roots. Sometimes we think of the three-year

---

1   Keith Watkins, *The Great Thanksgiving*, (St. Louis: Chalice Press, 1995), pp. 210-11.

Masters of Divinity program as matching the three years that Jesus is said to have spent with his disciples.

If ministry is a profession, what kind of profession is it? One could say that modern clergy have duties and expectations similar to those in the helping professions—medicine, social work, counseling. Although, clergy do engage in similar kinds of activities as these helping professions, these are not the only areas of engagement nor are then the predominant ones. For instance, as we've already noted clergy are teaching theologians, connecting them to another profession. Clergy are also engaged in management and leadership, linking them to a still different profession. The reason why the Academy of Parish Clergy exists is that the founders of the organization understood this to be a professional vocation.

While there is much to be said for the idea of professionalism in ministry, there has been significant pushback in recent years. In part this pushback stems from a reexamination of the biblical understandings of the church and ministry. It also reflects dissatisfaction with institutional models of life. Although the idea of professional ministry would be a foreign concept to the authors of the New Testament, that doesn't invalidate this development. There is great value to be found in holding to professional standards, including appropriate knowledge base/education, ethics, and best practices.

Another cause of pushback is concern that the idea of professional ministry puts the emphasis on the wrong places—credentials, pensions, and salaries. It is not that those called to vocational ministry should not be paid, or even paid commensurate with their education and experience, but should not ministry be first understood theologically? If so, does a theological reflection on ministry lead to the conclusion that ministry is the equivalent of a helping profession?

Perhaps we can resolve some of these concerns by thinking of ministry as profession through a theological lens. Consider how Kathleen Cahalan frames the conversation:

Christian ministry is a profession that requires its members to profess a commitment to serve an ecclesial community, to represent that community and its members, and to conduct themselves in a way consistent with the religious claims of the group. This commitment is ritualized in the tradition of ordaining ministers.[1]

While there are standards and expectations, the focus is on service of God within an ecclesial community. It is the ecclesial community and not professional boards that hold clergy accountable.[2] But accountability, especially to standards of education/training and ethics is important. Consider the many scandals revealed in recent years—scandals that have included financial irregularities, sexual lapses, and abuse of power.

MINISTRY OUTSIDE THE ECCLESIAL COMMUNITY

The book carries the title *Out of the Office*, which serves as a reminder that ministry often occurs outside the confines of the congregation, or at the very least outside the confines of the church building. There are, of course, ministries such as chaplaincies that serve institutional settings such as hospitals and prisons. Ministry within these institutions is an important expression of the compassionate nature of the Gospel. The ministries of those called to serve local congregations often extend beyond the confines of the congregation. That is, as John Wesley put it "the world is my parish." If the world is one's parish, how will that be lived out in practice? This is a question we will develop more fully later in the book. However, it is important for clergy to consider what role they have in public life. In answering such a question, one must always be aware of the dangers of becoming entangled with corrosive public structures. Nonetheless, how might one engage in prophetic minis-

---

1 Cahalan, *Introducing the Practice of Ministry,* p. 120.
2 If it is the ecclesial community and not professional boards that set standards, then we will need to consider the purpose of organizations like the Academy of Parish Clergy, which began life as a perceived equivalent to organizations like the American Medical Association.

try that contributes to the common good of all humanity? We will take this up in greater depth in a later chapter, but our definitions of ministry need to take into consideration this broader context.

ACTION AND REFLECTION:

If you are part of a faith community that has a policy on ordained ministry, access a copy, read it carefully, and look for the theological foundations that undergird the policy. Is it rooted in scripture, tradition, experience, and reason? Is it more rooted in organizational theory or theology?

Discussion:

1. What is your definition of ministry and how did you derive it?

2. What is the difference between vocational ministry and lay ministry? How does the idea of the priesthood of all believers fit into this conversation?

3. Compare the definitions of ministry offered by the Faith and Order Commission's *Baptism, Eucharist, and Ministry* document and that offered by Tony Jones. What are the similarities and what are the differences? How might these two visions of ministry and the church influence church structure?

4. What are the ways in which church structure and ministry are understood in the New Testament? How should our reading of the New Testament influence the way we understand ministry (if one is a Christian)?

5. In what ways, might we view ministry as a profession? How does professional status influence the way we understand ministry?

6. How might ministry be undertaken outside the confines of the church? What forms might it take and how should we understand this ministry theologically?

Chapter 3

Giftedness and Ministry

We can't talk about a call to ministry without talking about giftedness. A theology of ministry must reflect upon the biblical witness to the variety of gifts that have been poured out on the Body of Christ. Looking at ministry from a pneumatological perspective, we're led to the Pauline concept of the *charism*, or gift of grace. When we spend time with Romans 12, 1 Corinthians 12, 14, and Ephesians 4, we encounter a variety of gifts that enable the whole people of God to engage in ministry. At the same time, we discover that some gifts seem to empower certain persons to take on responsibilities of teaching and leadership within the community. The key point is that like a body, the Body of Christ has many members, and each member of the body has its place and purpose.[1]

All are Gifted

In the King James translation of Ephesians 4:11-12 we get a reading that has influenced generations of Christians regarding ministry.

> [11] And he gave some, apostles; and some, prophets; and some, evangelists; and some, *pastors and teachers;*
> [12] For the perfecting of the saints, *for the work of the ministry*, for the edifying of the body of Christ:

The comma separating "for the perfecting of the saints" and "for the work of the ministry" reflected the belief that pastors and teachers did "the work of the ministry," rather than perfecting the saints for ministry. A comma can make a big difference. However,

---

1 I explore the idea of giftedness in depth in my book *Unfettered Spirit.* For a discussion of Ephesians 4 see Cornwall, *Ephesians*, p. 48-54.

if we remove the comma then these gifts of apostleship, prophetic ministry, evangelism, pastoring/teaching are designed to equip the saints so that they can engage in ministry. The unfortunate result of allowing the comma to influence our theology of ministry is that it leads both clergy and laity to assume that clergy are hired to do ministry on behalf of the church. But, that doesn't seem to make sense of the text.[1]

If we start with the premise that everyone is gifted by the Spirit, then we can all move toward discovering our call to ministry. If we recognize that all are gifted and that these gifts differ from person to person, then perhaps we can begin narrowing the gap that separates clergy and laity. It's important to recognize that those who are called to what is termed vocational ministry are not more gifted than those we term laity, they're just differently gifted. Even among clergy, while all are gifted not all are gifted in the same way. Because of this, those who serve congregations will engage in their ministries in different ways. Since all Christians are by virtue of their giftedness ministers, though they don't all share the same ministry, it would be inappropriate to assume that the work of the laity is any less a form of ministry than that which is engaged in by the professionals.

As a pastor, I know that pastors serve a very important function in the life of the church. Due to their training and often giftedness, they offer an important service to the church, but their work is not the totality of the church's ministry. Another way of asking this question would be: What aspects of church life should be considered off limits to lay people?[2] In answering this question, should we not envision the following as expressions of the total ministry of the church: teaching Sunday school, visiting the homebound,

---

1 There is, of course, no comma in the source text. It is supplied by the translators based on their interpretation of the text.

2 It is appropriate that I confess to be a member of a faith community that does not limit the celebration of the sacraments to the clergy. In the Disciples tradition both clergy and lay elders celebrate the Lord's Supper. See Keith Watkins, ed., *Thankful Praise: A Resource for Christian Worship,* (St. Louis: CBP Press, 1987), 15-16.

leading grief groups, serving meals to the homeless, marching for civil rights, evangelizing our neighborhoods, or preaching, are these not all forms of ministry whether we do these as laity or clergy?

Whatever form ministry takes; it is an act of service, as is suggested by the Greek word we translate as ministry (*diakonos*). This Greek word can be translated in a variety of ways, as can be seen from reading Scripture, but one of its most important translations is that of servant. Jesus offers us a very pertinent model of servant leadership when he bowed down before his disciples and washed their feet (John 13). We see this example also present in Paul's description of Jesus as the one who emptied himself, taking on the form of the servant, a posture that we are encouraged to take on ourselves (Philippians 2:9-15).

PRIESTLY ROLES

The word "minister" connotes a call to service, and all ministry is service. However, there are other terms/roles to be found in Scripture, which need to be explored. One of these roles is that of priestly ministry. Traditionally a priest is a person set aside for spiritual work, especially with regard to assisting in the divine-human relationship. One might go to a temple or church and request a divine blessing from a priest. In many Christian traditions, the efficacy of the Eucharist or baptism are related to the priest/minister's status as one ordained in apostolic succession.

When one reads the New Testament, it appears that such mediators are unnecessary. Since Jesus is our high priest he alone serves as our mediator with God, and therefore whatever priestly work needs to be done each person can do for themselves. We are empowered to intercede not only for ourselves but for our neighbors as well (Hebrews 10). We are also members of a royal priesthood (1 Peter 2:5-9). If all followers of Christ are part of this royal priesthood, then this would seem to eliminate the clergy as necessary priestly intermediaries. Each believer whether lay or clergy are invited to join in the priestly service of intercession. Therefore, as one of the founders of my own tradition once wrote, "whatever constitutes *the worship of* God is the common privilege of all the disciples *as such*."[1] As disciples of Jesus, baptized by the Spirit, we are servants and priests for all people, and thereby we are freed to join in the full ministry of God.

VARIETY OF GIFTS AND CALLINGS

To say that all are servant ministers and priests does not mean that we all have the same roles and callings. The lists of spiritual gifts that we find in the letters of Paul (recognizing questions about the authorship of Ephesians) provide sufficient diversity that it's clear that these lists are only suggestive of possibilities and not final or normative lists. Among those listed gifts, however, are gifts that speak to the need for order within the community. Even as ships need pilots to navigate difficult waters, communities of faith require persons able to pilot the congregation. Within the community there are those who are gifted for leadership, and in time—if congregations are spiritually aware—these gifts will be recognized and affirmed. Considering this reality, there is a place for the one called to vocational (professional) ministry. However, this recognition of the role of the vocational minister does not relieve the laity of their ministerial callings.

In the process of discovering one's spiritual gifts, one needs to discern when and where these gifts should be used. The community will, if it is listening to the Spirit, help us discern the answer to this question. The process of discernment is aided by trying out a variety of ministry roles, even if these roles seem to lie beyond what we consider to be our own gifts. When I became a pastor, one area of ministry that I didn't feel comfortable with was that of the pastoral care of the sick and dying. In time, however, as I gained more experience, I discovered that I was sufficiently equipped to provide effective pastoral care. Thus, as Kathleen Cahalan notes:

---

1   Royal Humbert, ed., *Compend of Alexander Campbell's Theology*, (St. Louis: Bethany Press, 1961), p.175.

Charisms are gifts that rarely come perfectly formed and ready for action. They usually come as a seed, to use Jesus' metaphor, and they need a great deal of healthy soil and tending to become fully mature (Mark 4:3-9). [1]

Knowing that all are gifted, but gifted differently, and that charisms do not come fully formed, but require development, then can we say that whatever we do as the people of God is really an expression of the reign of God? Therefore, as we join in the work of ministry we participate in God's work of expanding the realm of God in this world, claiming spiritual territory for redemption.[2]

ACTION AND REFLECTION:

Access a spiritual gifts inventory and fill it out. What gifts are revealed? How might the suggested gifts influence the way you do ministry or conceive of ministry?

Discussion:

1. How does a comma in Ephesians 4 impact the way we understand ministry? Are clergy called to equip the saints for ministry or do ministry for the saints?

2. What is gift-based ministry? How do gifts (charisms) impact the way we engage in ministry?

3. Clergy are often understood to be priests, or mediators of the divine-human relationship. How does a gift-based understanding of ministry influence the way we understand priestly ministry?

1 Cahalan, *Introducing the Practice of Ministry,* p. 119.
2 Jürgen Moltmann, *The Church in the Power of the Spirit: A Contribution to Messianic Ecclesiology*, Margaret Kohl, trans. (New York: Harper and Row, Publishers, 1977), pp. 302-4.

4. How might we understand the varieties of gifts and ministries? How might ordained/vocational ministry relate to other forms of ministry?

5. Should we expect ministry gifts to be fully formed, or will use/ practice help us develop them?

CHAPTER 4

MINISTRY AND THE MISSIONAL CHURCH

I gave this book the title *Out of the Office*, in part because it reflects my own commitment to be missionally-engaged. The word missional has come into wide use in recent years, as Christian congregations have begun to recognize that the old "attractional" model of church life no longer works. People aren't going to church out of civic or religious duty. Facing greater competition from the broader culture for time, money, and energy, religious communities across the spectrum are face the challenge of engaging a community that increasingly finds religious institutions irrelevant. It is in this context, as congregations look inside and outside, that the missional movement holds promise for the future.

There are critics of the missional movement, and some have suggested that the term has been so widely used that it has lost its meaning. It is possible that this word, like many words, is used too broadly to have real meaning, but if we look to it is origins we may find a way forward. The missional ideal invites us to see mission as being more than "outreach," which usually involve financial contributions to good works that others engage in either at home or across the globe. The missional ideal invites us to rethink what it means to be a congregation and see all that we do in missional terms. Whether it's education or worship or fellowship or service, they all are rooted in the call to bear witness to God's work in the world, a work we participate in both in the church building and outside it.

In the two chapters that follow, we will explore ways in which the world (both physical and virtual worlds) is our parish. This idea that goes back at least to John Wesley, who wrote in his journal

the justification for his ministry that often transgressed the rules
of the day:

> "I look upon all the world as my parish; thus far I mean,
> that, in whatever part of it I am, I judge it meet, right, and
> my bounden duty to declare unto all that are willing to hear,
> the glad tidings of salvation. This is the work which I know
> God has called me to; and sure I am that His blessing attends
> it. Great encouragement have I, therefore, to be faithful in
> fulfilling the work He hath given me to do. His servant I am,
> and, as such, am employed according to the plain direction of
> His Word, 'As I have opportunity, doing good unto all men';
> and His providence clearly concurs with his Word; which has
> disengaged me from all things else, that I might singly attend
> on this very thing, 'and go about doing good.'"[1]

Wesley's vision has missional implications for the way we engage in ministry. It is not a matter of competing for bodies to place
in the pews. Rather it is a call to bear witness to the good news of
salvation, recognizing that salvation means more than gaining a
seat in heaven after death.

As we ponder the realms where ministry will take place, it is
important as well to remember that the value of the institutional
church is being called into question by growing numbers of our
neighbors. In fact, the value of institutions is being called into
question. While I understand the criticism leveled at institutions
(they can become rigid and unresponsive), I count myself as one
who affirms the value and need for community, which usually ne-
cessitates some form of institution. Perhaps the problem is not the
institution per se, but the way we understand the purpose of the
institution. Is the institution the end or the means to an end? If it
is the latter, then can it become the vehicle of the Spirit through
which the realm of God is revealed in the world? The temptation
that congregations face is becoming little more than a social club

---

1   John Wesley, "Journal of John Wesley," *Christian Classics Ethereal Library*,
     (http://www.ccel.org/ccel/wesley/journal.vi.iii.v.html

or service organization. When that happens, it ceases to be the body of Christ.

When we envision ministry from a missional perspective, we will ask how the church is perceived by those living outside its walls. Does the world look at the church and see Christ, or does it see a group of self-righteous, self-satisfied people intent on protecting their religious turf, and who have little of Christ's love within them? Taking a missional view of ministry assumes that the congregation's mission has both inward and outward expressions, which need to be aligned.

Ministry today occurs in a vastly different context than in ages past. The Christian church is no longer a dominant player in the western culture that most readers of this book inhabit. North America and Europe have become more diverse ethnically and religiously. We live in a pluralistic age, where people of different traditions encounter each other regularly. They might even be married to each other. So, while Christianity is blossoming in Latin America, Africa, and Asia, it's losing its grip on Europe and North America. Church attendance has been on the decline for decades. Among Millennials (ages 18-35), the fastest growing religious demographic is known as "nones." This is not because they necessarily reject faith in God, they just don't see the point of religious institutions. If this is true for Millennials, what about the next generation that is coming on the scene at this very moment.

It should not surprise anyone that clergy have also suffered in reputation. In earlier years, clergy might not have been well paid, but they were held in high esteem by society at large. With the collapse of Christendom, clergy have largely lost their prior role as the religious conscience of the community. Clergy may still be called on to pray at city council meetings and other events, but it's mostly a remnant of earlier practices. Indeed, it can be an expression of a civil religion that has little theological foundation.

In places like the United States where religion is disestablished, religion is understood largely in consumer terms. Church growth occurs when congregations follow the lead of Starbucks and give religious seekers a good experience. Good music, preaching, and program, it is believed, will contribute to the success of a congregation. But what happens to community when professional excellence is held up as the goal of the institution. What happens to those who don't "measure up"? In an age of big box stores, big box churches thrive, but how long will they continue to thrive? What happens when tastes change? Consider that most mega-churches are conservative, while younger generations are more liberal, especially on social mores, including welcoming LGBTQ persons into all walks of life, including the church.

Growing numbers of people in Europe, Australia, and North America describe themselves as being spiritual but not religious. In many ways, this is the next stage in consumerist religion. In such a vision, there is no need for an institution, because spirituality is a personal/private enterprise. So instead of a congregation, you go to a bookstore or the internet, and create your own form of spirituality. In such a vision, where does one engage the world in a way that is transformative?

What this means is that congregations and clergy need to be adaptable. But if they're to adapt, how is this adaptation to be grounded? This is where our theology of ministry comes into play. As we wrestle with adapting to these changes, we need to examine the locus of ministry. Once the locus of ministry/mission was the parish, and the parish was a neighborhood. Before disestablishment, there was, at least officially, only one faith body responsible for the spiritual life of the community. Disestablishment dispersed the work, which in turn led to competition, and consumerism. A missional understanding of the church's responsibility ultimately leads back to the parish idea. The question is how do we get there in a theologically responsible way?

This is not the place to fully explore what it means to be a parish in our modern context. The idea of the parish has roots in Christendom. Each neighborhood or village had its parish, supported by the state, and everyone was expected to worship in that context. To do otherwise was to be a non-conformist, and nonconformists endangered the state and thus were frowned upon. So, if we're to re-envision the parish in a missional context, it will need to take on a new identity. In this new context, there may be different expressions of faith planted in a community, but they don't see each other as competitors, but as partners. These communities reach out and connect to other neighborhoods. The key here is to understand that the missional ideal is connected to place. It's embodied in the daily lives of the people who make up the congregation. There is a connectedness between professions of faith in worship and daily life.[1]

Another factor to consider in moving toward a missional vision is the fact that people no longer go to church out of duty, or at least very few do so. So, faith must involve more than cultural expectations. What is interesting is that even in the midst of institutional decline there are signs of spiritual revival or awakening. This spiritual awakening is taking a variety of forms.[2] It is in this context of this new emerging spiritual awakening that those called to ministry engage in their ministry—not so much as religious professionals, but as spiritually-gifted persons set aside to equip and lead missional communities.

At a basic level, the missional principle teaches us that whereas earlier generations sent out missionaries, in this new vision the local congregation is itself an agent of God's mission in the world. It is a movement that calls on the church to move beyond seeing mission as something the church "does" to understanding that mission is what the church "is."

---

1 For a helpful conversation about the idea of parish see Paul Sparks, Tim Soerens, and Dwight Friesen, *The New Parish: How Neighborhood Churches are Transforming Mission, Discipleship and Community,* (Downers Grove: IVP Books, 2014).

2 Diana Butler Bass has written in detail about this spiritual awakening in her book *Christianity After Religion: The End of Church and the Birth of a New Spiritual Awakening,* (San Francisco: Harper One, 2012).

MISSIONAL THEOLOGY AND THE NATURE OF MINISTRY

To be missional is to discern where God is at work and then let that understanding shape the ministry of the church. Ministry in this vision is both Spirit-led and Spirit-empowered. The missional church is therefore truly charismatic. That is, ministry in the church is rooted in the spiritual gifts present in the community.[1]

Craig Van Gelder, a leading missional theorist, lays out the missional principle in the form of a syllogism:

The Church *is*.
The Church *does* what the church *is*.
The Church *organizes* what it *does*. [2]

He writes that "the key point to understand is that the Spirit-led ministry of the church flows out of the Spirit-created nature of the church."[3] Therefore, "being" precedes "doing." What the church "does" and how it organizes itself should reflect the church's essence as the agent of God's redemptive mission in the world. In focusing on the church's essence, this movement challenges one of Protestantism's greatest weaknesses—its lack of a strong ecclesiology. To suggest that in an anti-institutional age we need to attend to ecclesiology may sound rather foolish, but if we're to move into a new reality where being leads to doing, then we'll need to rethink what it means to be church.

Focusing on *being* rather than *doing* might seem to lead to passivity, but to be missional is not to be passive. Mission is what the church is and thus what it does. That means that mission is more than simply giving money to charitable organizations. Mission may look at times like charitable actions, but it is much more than this. Mission may involve good works, but by engaging in this work the presence of God in the world is being revealed. It is incarnational.

---

1 Cornwall, *Unfettered Spirit: Spiritual Gifts for the New Great Awakening.*
2 Craig Van Gelder, *The Ministry of the Missional Church: A Community Led by the Spirit.* Foreword by Alan J. Roxburgh. (Grand Rapids: Baker Books, 2007), p. 12.
3 Van Gelder, *Ministry of the Missional Church*, p. 18

Once again, theology comes into play, because too often churches look like service clubs with a religious veneer. They do good things, but their good things seem disconnected with their faith.

The missional church is not insular. That is, while it attends to the spiritual welfare of the gathered community, it is also committed to being engaged in the world beyond its walls. To be missional isn't an either/or proposition. It is a both/and proposition. To become this kind of missional community will mean that things can get messy. The ideal of "institutional effectiveness," if such effectiveness is understood to be growth in numbers, misses the church's divine calling to be an agent of reconciliation. Numerical growth may or may not occur, but that shouldn't affect the way one perceives one's calling. Instead, it seeks to live "into all that the Triune God intends the church to be in the light of its creation by the Spirit."[1] That purpose is the redemption/transformation of the world. Such a vision requires deep theological reflection on the ministry of the church, for those called to ordained ministry in this context are not called simply to do ministry for others, but to engage in ministry with others as they live out this transformative faith in the world.

"Spirit-led ministry" is rooted in God's act of "reconciling the world to himself" (2 Corinthians 5:19). The church becomes missional when it becomes a community of reconciled diversity that is led by the Spirit into the world to unmask the powers through suffering service. To accomplish this goal one must recognize that the context for doing ministry is ever changing. While the mission may not change, the way it is done will change. The image Van Gelder offers here is that of the church continually "forming" (missional) and "reforming" (confessional). That is, the Reformation principle that the "church is always reforming" (*semper reformanda*), that it is always reengaging with its heritage must be balanced with contextualization— "the church is always forming" (*semper formanda*). These two poles keep the church in a creative tension, so that it is both rooted in its heritage and able to engage its context. To do so effectively will, of course take great skill and awareness.

1   Van Gelder, *Ministry of the Missional Church*, p. 182.

To guide this effort at being missional in context, Craig Van Gelder lists seven aptitudes. Spirit-led missional congregations must: 1) "learn to read a context as they seek their contextuality." This includes both sociological and theological readings. 2) They must "anticipate new insights into the gospel." They will seek to discern the fuller meaning of the gospel by listening for indigenous voices. 3) They will "anticipate reciprocity" —that is, they should expect to be changed by the encounter with the context. 4) They will "understand they are contextual, and, therefore, are also particular." While the missional church is "catholic" it is also very "local" —embedded in a particular context. There can be, therefore, no one size fits all programs or even "model congregations." 5) It must understand that ministry is always contextual and, therefore, is also practical." It must develop specific practices that are rooted in its time and place. 6) It will "understand that doing theology is always contextual and, therefore, is also perspectival." Theology is rooted in long held confessions of faith, but these confessions must be understood in their particular context and culture. Thus, there is, he says, "no universal confession." We must learn to confess the faith anew in our own context, translating themes, beliefs, and ideas. Finally, 7) we must "understand that organization is always contextual and, therefore, is also provisional." This assumption affirms what we know to be true already in the way the church is present in the New Testament. Even in the first century the church expressed itself in different ways depending on where it was located. As time passed and the church moved outward into the world it adapted to new surroundings, and continues to do so to this day. The organizational form the church takes will reflect its surroundings. This is good news, according to Van Gelder, because "congregations are able to relate to any culture and to any context."[1]

Van Gelder suggests that American church life has taken on three primary forms: established, corporate, and missional, with most contemporary churches being corporate." That is, they see themselves as existing to accomplish something for God on a

---

1   Van Gelder, *Ministry of the Missional Church*, pp. 63-67

voluntary basis. Focus here is on function and is defined by organizational views and values. Throughout the history of America,
this church has taken on various guises, often guided by business or
governmental theory. The "corporate" model has, he believes, run
into a major wall in the last several decades. This wall is the growing
anti-institutionalism present in western society. Thus, traditional
denominations have begun to struggle.

Into the void has stepped this new model, one less focused
on church growth or effectiveness—including seeker and pur-
pose-driven models—and more on the mission of God (*missio dei*)
or the redemptive reign of God. The author pushes us on further
toward being congregations that are "missionary by nature" and
participating "in God's mission in the world."

MISSIONAL MINISTRY – SKILLS AND APTITUDES

Missional ministry requires distinct skills and aptitudes in discernment, decision-making, and organization. This work requires
new ways of looking at scripture and doing theological education
(however, I need to interject here that as we reform theological
education, we need to be careful that we don't move away from
theological formation as a primary value and move simply to vocational training). Strategy and skills are important, but they need
to be theologically grounded so that God is kept at the forefront.
We must always be wary of the tendency to so "professionalize" the
church that it looks more like a business than the Body of Christ.
Action is to be guided by both biblical theology and sociological
theory—always keeping in mind the spiritual foundations of the
community.

As for organizing principles, many new missional communities are rejecting closed systems such as bureaucracy, and instead
opting for more organic ("open-systems") models. Whatever system or process adopted, moving forward through the twenty-first
century will involve the ability to adapt to new contexts and new
opportunities. Constitutions are important, but interpreting them

may require some flexibility (think midrash). Again, this is why theology is so important to ministry. If we focus merely on process and policy, we face the possibility of getting mired in quickly out-moded methodologies. By focusing on a theology of ministry, we can evaluate methods that emerge, asking whether they will fulfill the purpose of ministry. There is a tendency in religious circles to baptize current organizational models—in my denomination the "functional church" model emerged in the 1940s, and in many ways that model continues to guide congregational life to this day, even though congregations have become overburdened by the de-mands of the model, because this is the way things have been done and therefore must be done. By looking at organizational models theologically, we can be discerning in our attempts to reform the way we do church.

It is helpful to discern where organizational models originate. Thus, the ministry of episcopacy in the first century evolved into something very different a few centuries later that reflected the or-ganizational model of the Roman Empire. The democratic values of my own denomination reflect the values of early nineteenth century America. There's nothing wrong with this if we recognize that what we're doing is adapting current organization models for a religious purpose and that they're not theologically determined.

Whatever organizational model we choose will need to be judged based on how it fits our understanding of God's mission of redemptive love for the world. With this in mind, we can turn to the Book of Acts and use it as a lens to examine how change and growth interrelate. But was we do this we can't simply try to replicate the Book of Acts in our day. The movement with which I am affiliated tried that without much success. In planning for change, we should remember that if change structures we're not changing core values. We're simply aligning structures with those core values. What we discover by looking at the Book of Acts, is that a variety of models of congregational life came into existence that were culturally appropriate.

In a missional understanding of the church, the church is called now and in the future to attend to its calling, which is, Van Gelder notes, "living into all that the Triune God intends the church to be in light of its creation by the Spirit. The church created by the Spirit is missionary by nature. It is called, gathered, and sent into the world to participate fully in God's mission."[1] Thus, we begin with the church as it is and discover that what it does and how it organizes what it does, is rooted in what it is.

ACTION AND REFLECTION:

Take some time to envision how one's congregation can embody the missional spirit. Then, perhaps with a team, envision and lay out a plan for engaging in ministry that takes the congregation out into the world, not only financially, but bodily. That is, find a way to get one's "hands dirty," and then reflect on it theologically.

Discussion:

1. What does it mean to be a "missional" community or congregation?

2. How does a missional church differ from a corporate church?

3. How is what the church does related to what the church is?

4. How is mission different from charity?

5. What is the danger of becoming inwardly focused and insular?

6. What are the theological foundations for missional ministry?

---

1 Van Gelder, *Ministry of a Missional Church,* p. 182

CHAPTER 5

THE WORLD IS OUR PARISH

If we affirm a missional model of ministry, in which the world itself is the parish, how do identify our place in that ministry? If you're called to be a shepherd, where will you find your flock? Is it only among the church membership, or should you cast your vision much wider? Those called by congregations to serve as vocational ministers are charged with caring for the congregation. This is the foundational community for one's ministry. Even those called to be apostles and evangelists (Ephesians 4:11), are rooted in and responsible to a community. There are responsibilities requiring one's attention in the congregation, including preaching, teaching, and pastoral care. But, what about those living outside the congregation? What responsibility does one have for them?

Could it be that the world is our parish, or at least a portion of the world? At some point or another, a clergyperson will be asked to minister to persons outside the congregation. It could be a funeral or a wedding. It might be a hospital visit or a visit to the death bed. It could also involve engagement in prophetic ministry, such as the one engaged in by Dr. Martin Luther King or more recently by Rev. Dr. William Barber.[1]

CONGREGATIONS AND THE COMMUNITY

One model of ministry that might be helpful in envisioning engaging the broader community is congregation-based community organizing, which has many of the same characteristics as the

---

1   William J. Barber II with Jonathan Wilson-Hartgrove, *The Third Reconstruction: Moral Mondays, Fusion Politics, and the Rise of a New Justice Movement*, (Boston: Beacon Press, 2016).

Civil Rights Movement that was rooted in congregations. When one enters such a ministry in the community, one doesn't go alone. The point of such ministry is to engage the congregation in pursuing the common good through advocacy. Community organizing seeks to connect one's self-interest with the self-interests of others in pursuit of justice. Having been involved in congregation-based community organizing, I know that this kind of ministry can be risky, especially for clergy in suburban communities where religion and politics are a bit like oil and water. They don't mix. In congregations that are politically diverse, what looks like politics can be divisive. Not only that, since community organizing seeks to channel righteous anger into advocacy for others, how does such an attitude fit with calls to love others? While these are concerns, we also know that there are human beings in need of support as they seek justice. But, how might congregations engage in the pursuit of justice? What are the theologically-rooted values that can guide this work, lest the church simply becomes the religious arm of a political party?

Community organizing is one way to engage the broader community. There are other ways that might include service as a volunteer chaplain to first responders, or perhaps as an on-call minister at a hospital. Having accepted a call to serve as a police chaplain, the duties of such a calling include ministry to officers and staff, but also may involve tending to the spiritual needs of the community in times of tragedy and crisis. These are all expressions of ministry that take place beyond the congregation, but are undertaken as extensions of the congregation's ministry in the world.

There was a time when clergy, like physicians, made house calls. A pastor I worked with after college (I was the youth minister) in a rural area visited every congregant each month. He didn't stay long, but every afternoon he made ten or more calls. There may still be clergy like this, especially in small towns and rural areas, but less so in suburban and urban areas. Some clergy simply make sure they're in the office in case members stop in. But the number of people stopping by with any regularity for conversation continues to decrease. It's more likely that such conversations will take place at a coffee shop or some other external venue. So, to do ministry one will likely have to go out into the field, where people are living their daily lives.

While this is the reality we face, how do we understand this broader sense of ministry theologically? It must be more than a strategy if it is to be true to one's calling. One place to start is with the words of Jeremiah: "Promote the welfare of the city where I have sent you into exile. Pray to the Lord for it, because your future depends on its welfare" (Jeremiah 29:7 CEB). Whether we see ourselves as exiles or not, in many ways this is a plausible vision of our place in the world. The calling is clear—we are to "promote the welfare of the city." When Jeremiah spoke these words to fellow exiles living in Babylon, he was reminding them of their responsibility for their neighborhood. He didn't encourage them to hunker down and turn inward. He pointed their attention outward, to the needs of the community.

MISSIONAL MINISTRY AND COMMUNITY ORGANIZING

Returning to the missional calling, we could envision community organizing as on facet of missional engagement. Churches have long been engaged in charitable actions, but there are limits to its value. Charitable work often treats symptoms rather that getting to the heart of matters.

Having brought up the concept of congregation-based community organizing, I would like to explore it more closely. The concept has been around for some time, but it became a topic of conversation when Barack Obama was first running for President in 2007. Much was made—pro and con—about him having been a community organizer early in his career. Some of his supporters responded by declaring that Jesus was himself a community organizer.

So, was Jesus a community organizer? If so, does this provide theological foundations for engaging in ministries of advocacy and solidarity? Can the principles of congregation-based or faith-based community organizing fit well with a missional understanding of the church?

Community organizing seeks to empower people who have been pushed to the margins by organizing them to advocate for solutions to neighborhood and community problems. Quite often, organizing efforts are undertaken by congregations, who join in coalitions. The principle here is that there is power in numbers, and if those who are marginalized are going to have their voices heard they need to come together. There are both secular and faith-based models of organizing. Faith-based organizers make use of other models, including that of Saul Alinsky, but it goes beyond the secular model. Alexia Salvaterierra and Peter Heltzel wrote that "faith-rooted organizing is based on the belief that many aspects of spirituality, faith traditions, faith practices and faith communities can contribute in unique and powerful was to the creation of just communities and societies."[1]

The principles of community organizing are easily translated into the work of ministry. As noted earlier, using one-on-one conversations, organizers seek to discern the concerns of community members, whether church-related or community-related. Congregations often will hold listening campaigns, where a group of church members are trained to conduct brief (thirty-minute) conversations with congregation members as well as members of the broader community (especially those living in the neighborhood of the congregation). After the team has these conversations, the teams compile a list of concerns, that are then brought to the coalition, so that the coalition can determine which issues are most pressing. From there, research and analysis is undertaken. Based on this research, teams begin to advocate for solutions. Having been trained in conducting one-on-one conversations, participants in community organizing can meet with community, political, and

---

1   Alexia Salvatierra and Peter Heltzel, *Faith-Rooted Organizing: Mobilizing the Church in Service to the World,* (Downers Grove, IL: Intervarsity Press, 2014), p. 9.

business leaders to press for the common good. Ultimately these principles are relational in nature.

Faith-rooted organizing, as an expression of the church's missional calling, is rooted in the prophetic tradition. Consider the work of Moses or Jeremiah. Jesus's own ministry is prophetic. He preached a vision of God's realm in which justice and righteousness would reign. The goal of faith-rooted organizing is not simply to build power, which is a major concern of traditional community organizing, but is to move toward the creation of the beloved community (a vision articulated by Martin Luther King, Jr.). A faith-rooted understanding of this work recognizes that this community is both present and future. Even our best efforts are complicated by the reality of sin and the lust for power. A theological perspective helps us keep the goal in mind, which is the unveiling of God's realm.

FINDING SPACE FOR MINISTRY IN THE WORLD

There has been much talk in recent years about the value of the local congregation for ministry in the world. Could it be that the institution has gotten in the way? On the other hand, arguments can be made and are being made that suggest that focusing on God's work in the world has hindered the building of true community, out of which ministry can unfold. One example of this latter vision is offered by John Nugent, who argues that the church is not called to make the world a better place, but rather to embody the realm of God in the world. As it does so it bears witness to God's vision of a better place. Nugent argues that the church's responsibility is to serve, as Israel did before, as a light to the world, living out God's kingdom principles, inviting others to join in.[1] This vision is different from the one outlined above, but it is a vision that needs to be considered as one discerns one's calling to be present in the world.

---

1 Nugent, *Endangered Gospel, passim.*

Even if one doesn't follow Nugent's lead on the connection of kingdom and congregation, there is value in reimagining the role of the congregation in the community. Especially in urban and suburban areas, congregations have been less focused on the neighborhoods and more on reaching a broader community. My own congregation, which is one of the few representatives of my denomination in the metro-Detroit area, attracts people from a thirty-mile radius, with most living beyond the five-mile radius (and we're a small congregation). But, what if we returned to the idea of the parish as our focus? That is the vision espoused by the Parish Collective and explored in some depth in the book *The New Parish*, written by the team of Paul Sparks, Tim Soerens, and Dwight Friesen. They seek to challenge the move to homogeneous, consumer-oriented, Christianity, to a recognition of the importance of presence and being rooted in a community, so that one might be in solidarity with one's neighbor. In their vision, there is some similarity to what John Nugent describes and there is discontinuity as well. The authors of this book make it clear that they're not advocating a return to the Christendom vision of parish, where the church was an expression of the government. At the same time, they envision the gathering of a community desiring to live missionally in neighborhood for the benefit of all.[1]

ACTION AND REFLECTION:

Set up a series of one-on-one conversations with members of the congregation. Invite them to share their sense of the state of the broader community. What issues concern them? How do they think they and the congregation might engage the broader community regarding these issues?

Discussion:

1.   How might the world be the parish for clergy/congregations?

---

1   Sparks, et al, *The New Parish, passim.*

2. What might congregations learn about ministry in the community from community organizing efforts? How is such work different from political activity? How is it grounded theologically?

3. What are other ways in which congregations/clergy can engage in mission/ministry in the world?

4. How might we recapture the idea of the parish in a post-Christendom era?

CHAPTER 6

THE VIRTUAL WORLD IS OUR PARISH

In the previous chapter, we explored ways in which the world is our parish. Recognizing the importance of community, we were reminded that a visible presence in the broader community can offer it a source of grace and hope. That said, living as we do in a digital age, the community in which we are present is much larger than we might previously have allowed. The question is how we might engage the virtual world as congregations and as clergy? What are the resources out there that might aid is in the discernment process?

UNDERSTANDING THE VIRTUAL WORLD

The virtual world is the world of the internet, of social media, and the smartphone. We live in it, whether we like it or not. Most clergy have a computer, and they likely have access to the internet. Many have a smart phone, which connects them digitally not only to their congregations, but also to this larger virtual world. From what I can see from conversations on places like *Facebook*, many clergy have a love/hate relationship with the virtual world. That is likely because once we're drawn in, it can consume us. Still, the virtual world is upon us, as demonstrated by a President whose chosen media is *Twitter*.

In the Gospel of John, Jesus says that "God so loved the world, that he gave his only son, so that everyone who believes in him may have eternal life" (John 3:16). What is this world that God loves? After all, we're told in 1 John 2:15 not to love the world or the things of the world. In these two texts, we see how complex life in this world is, and that this complexity affects the way we do ministry. While the reading from 1 John may offer a cautionary

word, John 3:16 might be the better starting point. When we read
John 3, it is good to remember that the Greek word translated as
world in this passage is *kósmos*. That is, God loves the "cosmos."
In reflecting on this word, we can get the sense that God's love is
immense. It reaches beyond our barriers and boundaries.

One of the challenges that clergy face as we envision the idea
that the world is our parish is that the immensity of this world can
overwhelm us, especially if we broaden our concept of the world
to include the virtual. When we engage with the virtual world the
fast pace of change can also overwhelm us. What was relevant a year
ago, or five years ago, might be obsolete today, so how do we keep
up? To give an example of the pace of change, Christian and Amy
Piatt wrote a very helpful book about faith, virtual reality, and the
emerging generation. This book was published in 2007. That's only
ten years ago. It was a good book, and its basic message remains
true today. Unfortunately, its title is a bit dated—*MySpace to Sacred
Space: God for a New Generation*. *MySpace* was all the rage just a few
years ago (at the time the book was written), but unfortunately for
MySpace (and the book title), it was quickly surpassed by other sites
that attempted to do the same thing, only better. Thus, Facebook
replaced *MySpace* as the go to site. *MySpace* still exists, but only
for a very specialized market. Since *Facebook* doesn't want to suffer
the same fate, it continually reinvents itself, often to the chagrin of
its users (even tech-savvy ones). Despite the book's anachronistic
title, the Piatts make a good point: "Enter the antiquated behemoth
that is the modern church. Built on principles at least a century
old, many congregations, and even denominations are fighting to
remain relevant . . . The collective fear is that if the church doesn't
adapt to the digital shift, it will be left behind forever. But does
the church even belong in the digital world and vice versa?"[1] They
believe that we should, as people of faith, light a candle in this
virtual world. The question for congregations and clergy is how to
build a connection between physical congregations and this virtual

---

1   Christian Piatt and Amy Piatt, *MySpace to Sacred Space: God for a New
    Generation,* (St. Louis: Chalice Press, 2007), p.3.

world. It's not enough to build a website, set up a *Facebook* page, and perhaps add *Twitter* (not to mention all the other sites that keep joining the fray—I tried *Instagram*, but I still resist *Snapchat*).

MINISTRY IN A VIRTUAL WORLD

In an age when many prospective clergy are preparing themselves for their ministry online, it's not surprising that church exists online. The questions that get raised are often incarnational ones. How do you embody Christ in a virtual world? Even as we ask the questions ministry and religious life is burgeoning in the virtual realm.

There are numerous ways of doing ministry in the virtual world. There are worship services held in cyberspace utilizing such resources as *SecondLife*. An online congregation that has formed in my own denomination defines its vision in this way:

> Our VISION is to be a living network, crossing barriers and boundaries to connect the world with the Good News of God's redeeming love, revealed in Jesus Christ. (To us, this living network is the church, so when we say, "Net" we mean church. Net = Church. So…you may see us just say, "Disciples-Net" because "DiscipleNetChurch" seems repetitive.)[1]

Virtual congregations aren't meant to replace physical/brick and mortar congregations, but they can expand ministry, especially with those unable to attend a physical congregation.

While not every congregation will develop a virtual version of itself, the digital age offers important opportunities to minister to and with those who find it difficult to be with a brick and mortar community. Deanna Thompson, a Lutheran theologian, discovered the value of the virtual body of Christ as she battled cancer. Having resisted the virtual world to that point, she discovered a whole new support network as word got out through sites such as *CaringBridge* and even *Facebook*. She notes that it's not as if there weren't networks of prayer and support prior to the internet, it's

---

1 http://www.disciplesnet.org/about-us/misvis/

just that it has "exponentially increased the speed and scope of such connection."[1]

Another example of virtual ministry is described by Susan Cottrell in her book *Mom, I'm Gay*. Cottrell created the *FreedHearts* network to provide a safe space for families of LGBTQ persons to find support in a Christian context. This network uses *Facebook* groups to provide a supportive community when such support is not available from local Christian communities.[2]

There are likely many more such online communities that extend ministry to those in need or simply those who need community. That would include clergy, who often find it difficult to form supportive networks in their own backyard. There are many such entities on *Facebook* as well as other platforms.

A THEOLOGY OF VIRTUAL MINISTRY

While there are clear benefits to engage in virtual ministry, how should we ground this ministry theologically? There are good arguments for the priority of physical communities. James Thompson argues that the goal of pastoral ministry is the transformation of persons, and that this occurs within local communities. He writes that Paul's "focus on community formation is a welcome alternative to the focus on meeting the individual needs of members of the congregation. Moreover, his call for a communal and counter-cultural ethic provides a missing dimension in the contemporary understanding of ministry."[3] In Thompson's emphasis we see a response to the consumerist orientation of contemporary religion, where religious communities are set up to deliver spiritual goods for purchase. So, if we're going to expand ministry into the virtual

---

1   Deanna A. Thompson, *The Virtual Body of Christ in a Suffering World*, (Nashville: Abingdon Press, 2016), p. 4.

2   Susan Cottrell, *"Mom, I'm Gay": Loving Your LGBTQ Child and strengthening Your Faith*, Revised Edition, (Louisville: Westminster John Knox Press, 2016).

3   James W. Thompson, *Pastoral Ministry According to Paul: A Biblical Vision*, (Grand Rapids: Baker Academic, 2006), p. 29.

world, we'll want to keep this focus on transformation and community formation in mind. The purpose of such ministry is not simply to attend to individualist consumer trends, but to touch people's lives who may not have access to the kind of community that Thompson describes.

Deanna Thompson takes up the biblical image of the body of Christ as she lays out her vision of ministry to a suffering world. She affirms the vision of ministry articulated by James Thompson, but she also believes that it's possible to expand on Paul's vision of the body of Christ to include the virtual world. She reminds us that much of Paul's own ministry takes place virtually through his letters. She writes that "we see in Paul's virtual presence, leadership, and ministry communities at Corinth and beyond that care for all members was occurring through his letters and through the way in which those letters shape and sometimes correct the concrete practices of these church communities."[1] A good example of this virtual care on Paul's part can be found in a letter like his first epistle to the Corinthian church, which he wrote from a distance. Note the way he addresses that letter "to the church of God that is in Corinth, to those who are sanctified in Christ Jesus, called to be saints, together with all those who in every place call on the name of our Lord Jesus Christ, both their Lord and ours" (1 Corinthians 1:2). While the letter is sent to a particular church, it's good to remember that it existed in multiple sites, but it's also addressed everyone in every place who call on the name of the Lord. He addresses issues found in that congregation, but he does so in a way that can be used in other places and since it's now scripture in other times as well. Thus, contemporary Christians are included in Paul's virtual community.

Building on this vision of the virtual body of Christ, Deanna Thompson states that this body will always be a virtual body, because it "transcends specific, individual incarnations of the church." Despite the divisions that exist within the church catholic, it remains one body, so that "from the time of Paul onward, the church has also continued to turn to images like the body of Christ to

---

1   Thompson, *Virtual Body of Christ*, p. 42.

indicate that somehow, someway, Christians remain linked to one another beyond the boundaries of their local church communities or even their wider church bodies."[1]

By taking hold of the vision of the universal body of Christ, recognizing its virtual identity, we can begin to envision ministry taking place in a variety of formats. Using *CaringBridge*, for instance, we can keep in touch with persons whom it's difficult to connect with. As Deanna Thompson shares in her own testimony, there are times when a person simply is not up to having visitors in times of suffering. However, it's important to stay in touch. I've personally found Facebook to be an important resource for keeping in touch with congregants who are not able to get out and who are not able to receive visitors. Others have found *SecondLife* congregations to be a blessing because they provide a virtual experience for people who cannot get to services. The value of such experiences is that they keep people connected, even if virtually.

Not everyone is in a position to engage in such ministry, but it is an important way in which to expand ministry opportunities. It is a recognition that we are all connected virtually in some way with others. Bodies are important. The Christian faith is rooted in the idea that God took on a body (John 1:14). The question is how we remain embodied, even as we take that step into virtual ministry? With that question in mind, consider this prayer, based on St. Teresa of Avila's "Christ Has No Body." It is a revision provided by social media strategist Meredith Gould:

> Christ has no online presence but yours,
> No blog, no Facebook page but yours,
> Yours are the tweets through which love touches this world,
> Yours are the posts through which the Gospel is shared.
> Yours are the updates through which hope is revealed.
> Christ has no online presence by yours,
> No blog, no Facebook page but yours.[2]

---

1 Thompson, *Virtual Body of Christ*, p. 47.
2 Meredith Gould quoted in Thompson, *Virtual Body of Christ*, p. 71.

Such ministry is risky. It will require discernment. To be engaged online means being self-aware, recognizing that in the digital age we are more exposed than ever. So be careful about what you post and where you post!

To engage in ministry in the virtual world requires that one remember that standing at the center of the Christian faith, at least, is the promise of incarnation. As the Gospel of John declares, the Word became flesh and lived among humanity (John 1:14). There is a sense of uniqueness to that claim in John's gospel, but as Sallie McFague suggests it's possible to enlarge the vision:

> It is not the exclusive claim that matters, for one would assume that the source, power, and goal of the universe, its life and breath, its enlivening livening energy, would be embodied in many forms through its vast reaches. Rather, it is both the concrete, physical availability of God's presence ("became flesh") and the likeness to ourselves, a human being ("lived among us") that matter.[1]

As we explore the possibilities of creating spiritual communities in a virtual world, it's important that we remember that we are not disembodied spirits. We are embodied beings, flesh and blood entities, but at the same time we can embrace ministry to people and receive ministry virtually, if we remember that God meets us as embodied beings, even if the ministry occurs virtually. So, we might remember these words of Sallie McFague as words of guidance: "Within a Christic framework, the body of God encompasses compasses all of creation in a particular salvific direction, toward the liberation, healing, and fulfillment of all bodies. Thus, we can speak of the "cosmic" Christ, a metaphor for the scope of the body of God within a Christian framework."[2]

---

1   Sallie McFague. *The Body of God: An Ecological Theology,* (Minneapolis: Fortress Press, 1993), (Kindle Locations 2177-2180). Kindle Edition.
2   McFague. *The Body of God:* (Kindle Locations 2189-2190).

ACTION AND REFLECTION:

Take an assessment of your social media exposure, and that of the congregation you serve or participate in. In what ways are you engaging the virtual world? What forms does it take? How are these forms of social media engagement used in ministry? How does your theology of ministry inform this activity?

Discussion:

1. How has the advent of social media impacted ministry? What of the speed at which such forms of media change?

2. If we begin with the premise that social media is here to stay, how should congregations and clergy respond? What forms might such ministry take?

3. Deanna Thompson suggests ways in which we can theologically expand our understanding of the church as the body of Christ. How might Paul's virtual engagement with his congregations through letter writing serve to guide us in the contemporary world?

4. Following the lead of Sallie McFague, how do we engage the virtual world, while remaining embodied?

CHAPTER 7

THEOLOGY AND THE PRACTICES OF MINISTRY

We have been exploring what it means to engage in ministry outside the office, recognizing as Wesley declared, the "world is our parish." To affirm that principle does not mean that we neglect the community to which we are called. It is a both/and not an either/or calling. Having explored context for ministry it is appropriate to consider the practices of ministry, keeping in mind that both/and context.

In chapter three we examined the concept of gift-based ministry. We pondered the message of Ephesians, which declares that "each of us was given grace according to the measure of Christ's gift" (Ephesians 4:7). Ephesians mentions five gifts (assuming that pastor and teacher are separate giftings). These gifts are provided to the church so that the saints might be equipped "for the work of ministry, for building up the body of Christ, until all of us come to the unity of the faith and of the knowledge of the Son of God, to maturity, to the measure of the full stature of Christ" (Ephesians 4:11-13). When each part of the body is working properly, then the body is built up in love (Ephesians 4:16).

At one level, every Christian is called to participate in gift-based ministry. This is clear from 1 Corinthians 12 and 14. Ephesians, however, reminds us that in every community there will be those called to lead and equip the people of God to share in these varied ministries. In contrast to the professionalized vision of ministry that has developed over time, where congregations hire professionals to do ministry on their behalf, this vision assumes that all are called to ministry, and among those ministries are those that allow for leadership and equipping of the community to engage in ministry/mission wherever they find themselves in the world. Thus, as we move into the contemporary context, we understand that it is beneficial for congregations to set aside persons for this specialized calling. It is, with this in mind, that a mentoring pastor writes to a younger colleague telling him not to "neglect the gift that is in you, which was given to you through prophecy with the laying on of hands by the council of elders" (1 Timothy 5:11).

Those called to ordained ministry, and we'll talk more about this in a moment, are not responsible for all ministry tasks, but they are charged with equipping the congregation to share in ministry. Kathleen Cahalan identifies six basic practices of ministry, which we will look at in this chapter, reflecting theologically upon them. Cahalan offers a Christological interpretation, but we can also look at these tasks through a pneumatalogical lens.

TEACHING

The primary tasks of the teacher in the congregational context include equipping persons to take up ministries to which they are called and gifted, as well as passing on the tradition to others, especially those new to the faith. Theirs is a calling to interpret the faith, so that the people of God will be to discern the leading of God in their lives. We neglect this gift at our own peril. As theologian Joe Jones expressed it: "the church has fallen on ill times because it has gradually but definitely become *illiterate in the faith*. Through an almost imperceptible succession of compromises the church seems to have lost its roots, its bearings, and its hope."[1] He goes on to stress the importance of education to the full-orbed witness of the church in both word and deed.

When we look to the Gospels we see that Jesus was called rabbi for a reason. He was a teacher. He was an interpreter of the faith. In fact, he felt called to reinterpret the inherited faith in a way that would bring out its broader and deeper message for his own time. We see Jesus the teacher in action in the Sermon on the Mount. We also see Jesus the teacher at work in many of his healing acts.

---

1   Joe R. Jones, *On Being the Church of Jesus Christ in Tumultuous Times,* (Eugene, OR: Cascade Books, 2005), p. 11.

He healed on the Sabbath to remind the people that God set aside the Sabbath for the people and not as an end in itself. Thus, it was appropriate to heal on the Sabbath.

The minister expresses the gift of teaching by communicating knowledge and wisdom to others. Charisms linked to this practice include knowledge and understanding (knowing), use of language through speech and writing (doing), and humility (being). Cahalan notes that the teacher not only imparts knowledge, but also creates an environment for learning that "promotes discipleship."[1]

PREACHING

The ministry of preaching finds its roots in the prophetic tradition. The prophet proclaimed the message of God, calling on the people to attend to the Laws that God had established. Jesus was understood to have taken up this calling. Consider his affirmation of the word from Isaiah, that he is the one called to proclaim the good news (Luke 4:18-19). Cahalan notes that Jesus' prophetic message "called for people to make a decision, to live according to Yahweh's ways or to face destruction that comes from rejecting that path." In Jesus' vision of the ministry of preaching, the time for decision is now. What God demands is a radical conversion of heart and behavior.[2] She also notes that "preaching is a public act, a dialogical event between the preacher and the listeners."

In developing his own understanding of the role of the preacher, Karl Barth affirmed the principle that preaching became the Word of God when, rooted in Scripture, it bore witness to Jesus Christ, who was God's Word preeminent. William Willimon, reflecting on Barth's understanding of preacher notes: "Scripture keeps preaching theological because it is of the nature of scripture to speak primarily about God and only secondarily or derivatively about us."[3]

---

1   Cahalan, *Introducing the Practice of Ministry*, p. 74.
2   Cahalan, *Introducing the Practice of Ministry*, p. 76.
3   William Willimon, "Introduction," *The Word in this World: Two Sermons by Karl Barth*, Kurt I. Johanson, ed., (Vancouver, BC: Regent College Publishing, 2007), p. 13.

Thus, following this lead, can we not say that preaching is rooted in Jesus' own ministry, depends upon Scripture, and seeks to interpret that message to a new community, offering to it the good news that is to be found in Jesus Christ.

WORSHIP LEADERSHIP/PRAYER LEADER

Jesus wasn't a temple priest or the rabbi of a synagogue. He was an itinerant teacher and preacher, but he did lead his disciples in prayer and in worship. Worship was, as seen in his teaching on prayer (the Lord's Prayer) and his institution of the Lord's Supper, central to Jesus' understanding of discipleship. He not only challenged the powers and principalities, he also challenged the reigning forms of worship. Thus, he set in motion practices during his ministry that were picked up by later followers, centering on the Lord's Table.

In a more contemporary context, worship leadership includes leading of prayers, preaching, celebration of the sacraments. Some traditions reserve some roles, such as presiding at the Table to clergy. Other traditions, such as the Disciples of Christ, allow for non-clergy to take on such roles, including presiding at the Table.

PASTORAL CARE

One of the primary areas of ministry that parish clergy take up is pastoral care. This calling includes a variety of tasks including the visitation of shut-ins and those who are in the hospital. It involves tending to the dying and comforting those who grieve. A healthy body or community requires that attention be given to those experiencing spiritual, emotional, and physical issues, though in a healthy community this work is taken up not only by clergy but the congregation as a whole (one expression of this is the Stephen Ministry).

Jesus exemplified this form of ministry as he engaged the ministry of healing. Stories of Jesus the healer are prominent in the gospels, and they are closely linked to his preaching. The healings he engaged in were embodiments of his proclamation of the good news.

The ministry of pastoral care is also rooted in the biblical image of the shepherd. The shepherd is one who cares for and protects the sheep. In the context of the faith community, this work of shepherding involves watching over those in trouble and distress. Cahalan notes that this ministry is usually seen as having four aspects—healing, sustaining, guiding, and reconciling. Healing involves bringing persons or groups of persons back to wholeness. The ministry of sustaining involves "accompanying those who experience loss." Guidance involves helping persons and communities engage in moral discernment—what should they do? Finally, reconciliation involves helping persons and groups forgive one another and themselves so that relationships with God and with others might be restored. These aspects of ministry involve such tasks as skilled advice, counseling, healing rituals, sacraments, charitable and social justice works, along with offering comfort, support, and encouragement. It is, therefore, a ministry of compassion for others.[1]

SOCIAL MINISTRY

It is clear that Jesus was concerned about those who lived on the margins. His own ministry was marked by acts of compassion, mercy, and justice. Cahalan notes that Jesus "preaches a message of radical love and forgiveness that neighbors are to extend to each other as God has extended to them."[2] Jesus' ministrations broke down barriers, such as his engagement with the Samaritan woman. He demonstrated what a ministry of servanthood might look like by washing the feet of his disciples. Jesus embraced ministry with the poor, as we see expressed in his parable of judgment in Matthew 25. The ministry of social justice involves a wide variety of practices from providing food, shelter, clothing, health care, prison ministry, but also addressing systemic issues that affect people. The

1 Cahalan, *Introducing the Practice of Ministry*, pp. 79-80.
2 Cahalan, *Introducing the Practice of Ministry*, p. 86.

minister is not called to be the sole provider of such ministry, but will both engage in it and leader others into ministries of service and advocacy on behalf of and with the poor and disenfranchised.

Social justice ministry is more than charitable actions, though it includes charitable acts. Social Justice ministry ultimately involves addressing the root causes of the problems being taken up by the congregation and its allies. As we have already noted, many congregations engage in congregation-based community organizing, which allows them to advocate for changes in the system that allows for problems to fester such as poverty and lack of access to proper mental health treatment. To engage the broader community in this way is political, but not necessarily partisan. Congregations might find allies that are partisan, but they should not become arms of those parties. So, if one is called to help lead such social ministries, their primary calling will to galvanize the community so that they might engage in service and providing the necessary means—educational, organizational, and financial—to help the church engage in ministry with those in need, no matter who they are or what their condition in life is.[1]

ADMINISTRATION

Vocational ministry involves leadership and administration. It is often said that Jesus didn't found an institution. This truism is rooted in fact, but perhaps misses the point. Jesus was, during his earthly existence, an itinerant preacher. He had a small band of followers, along with a few other supporters. Whatever organization that existed had to be flexible due to the kind of ministry in which he was engaged. Things began to change rather quickly as congregations were planted in Jerusalem and beyond. So, by the end of the first century, as witnessed in the New Testament books of Ephesians and the Pastorals, the church had begun to organize

---

1   Cahalan, *Introducing the Practice of Ministry,* p. 88. For an introduction to faith-based community organizing, see Kendall Clark Baker, *When Faith Storms the Public Square: Mixing Religion and Politics through Community Organizing to Enhance our Democracy,* (Cleveland: Circle Books, 2011).

itself to carry on ministry. Structures emerged to support an expanding ministry. It's not only the New Testament that suggests early organizational patterns. At a time when books that would later find their way into the scriptural record had yet to be written, we have firm statements about church leadership. Thus, Clement writes in the mid-90s CE as bishop of the church in Rome to the Corinthian church (again in disorder) offering words of guidance.

The apostles have preached the Gospel to us from the Lord Jesus Christ; Jesus Christ [has done so] from God. Christ therefore was sent forth by God, and the apostles by Christ. Both these appointments, then, were made in an orderly way, according to the will of God. Having therefore received their orders, and being fully assured by the resurrection of our Lord Jesus Christ, and established in the word of God, with full assurance of the Holy Ghost, they went forth proclaiming that the kingdom of God was at hand. And thus, preaching through countries and cities, they appointed the first-fruits [of their labours], having first proved them by the Spirit, to be bishops and deacons of those who should afterwards believe. Nor was this any new thing, since indeed many ages before it was written concerning bishops and deacons. For thus says the Scripture a certain place, "I will appoint their bishops in righteousness, and their deacons in faith."[1]

So, to say that Jesus didn't start a church, and therefore we needn't attend to administrative tasks is to fail to recognize evolving contexts. Yes, there are administrative tasks that need attention. That requires leaders, whether lay or clergy. Many clergy do not enjoy the administrative side of ministry, but whether one treasures these tasks, they will as most clergy ultimately discover find that administrative tasks take up considerable time and energy. Therefore, it is important to recognize the presence of God in these tasks. As Bruce and Katherine Epperly put it:

If we neglect the spiritual dimensions of administration, whether this involves dealing with church finances, property,

---

1   1 Clement 42, http://www.earlychristianwritings.com/text/1clement-roberts.html.

strategic planning, or personnel and organizational management, we will eventually jeopardize our ability to be effective spiritual leaders of our congregations. Recognizing that ministry is a holistic and interdependent enterprise calls us to move with prayerful agility through what may appear at first glance to be dissonant tasks.[1]

When congregations call pastors, they expect them to be leaders. The question is, what kind of leadership will they offer. There are many patterns of leadership and there is no one "biblical" pattern that must be preserved at all costs. However, we know that Jesus broke with traditional patriarchal family relationships. He did this be taking up the life of an itinerant preacher rather than stay home and take up the family business. Thus, in his own life, he shows us that discipleship involves a radical reorientation of human relationships. In this new way of life, we are called to a life of mutuality under God. In this context, there is an invitation to radical inclusiveness in relationship to one another. Thus, leadership is defined in non-hierarchical ways, or better—rather than engage in domination, leaders are called to servanthood. But to be a servant is not to be a doormat! Finding the necessary balance will take prayer and discernment.

When it comes to administrative leadership, we might look at some of Jesus' own statements, including some intriguing parables, such as the parable of the steward or household manager. He commended the steward who was faithful, wise, and prudent (Luke 16:1-9). He also praised the steward who was shrewd and diligent in "promoting and actualizing Christ's alternative vision of justice."[2] Paul also uses the idea of steward and servant in Galatians 4:1. The office of *episkopos* or overseer is essentially that of steward. Katherine Cahalan notes that, unfortunately, as the church moved into the second century it abandoned Jesus' reorientation of ad-

1   Bruce G. Epperly and Katherine Gould Epperly, *Tending to the Holy: The Practice of the Presence of God in Ministry,* (Herndon, VA: Alban Books, 2009), p. 120.
2   Cahalan, *Introducing the Practice of Ministry,* p. 93.

ministration/leadership and returned to a patriarchal model. We can, in our own time, move back toward the image of leadership offered by Jesus—one who leads but doesn't domineer. In rejecting the patriarchal model, we are in a better position to welcome the full range of ministerial gifts, including those of women, who have been historically excluded from ministry. If the surveys are correct, women still make far less than men.

There are other tasks that could be added, but these are foundational. We may have gifts that connect better to some tasks than others, but that doesn't mean we're not able to engage in them. Even those gifts that are evident within us need to be nurtured, and there are other tasks that will challenge us, but our gifts should enable us to engage in them. The important thing to remember here is that, if we take a gifts-based understanding of ministry, the church is healthiest when all members of the body are engaged.

ACTION AND REFLECTION:

Find a copy of the job description for the pastor (if in a multiple staff congregation, the job descriptions of all clergy) and take note of the listed responsibilities. How do you prioritize these duties? Why do you prioritize them as you do?

Discussion:

1. Of the responsibilities discussed above, which do you believe are primary and which are secondary? How do you make this determination? What is the theological basis?

2. How do these tasks relate to a theology of spiritual gifts? How do these tasks help build the body of Christ?

3. In the section on administration, mention was made of the presence of God in even the mundane tasks of administration and management. How might we extend what Bruce and Katherine Epperly say about administration to the entirety of one's tasks?

4. As you look at these tasks, do they require ordination, or can they be shared in by the laity?

CHAPTER 8

ORDINATION:
RECOGNITION AND AUTHORIZATION

If ministry is a shared vocation, then is there need for ordination? While not all faith communities ordain, the majority do ordain, though the various denominations have differing understandings and expectations. Some communities require episcopal ordination, while others require no official action. Some traditions restrict certain tasks to specific persons, while others are quite free. In most cases people are set aside for ministry through the laying on of hands, either by elders, fellow pastors, or by bishops. For some traditions, this act is an indelible mark that is not easily removed. For others ordination is simply a sign that one has certain responsibilities and ordination lasts as long as one is involved in this kind of business. Some traditions require great amounts of education while others have no specific requirements.

William Robinson, a British Disciple theologian, suggested that the foundations for Christian ministry are to be found in the ministry of the apostles. The commission given to the Apostles, as he understood it, was not given to them alone but to all whom they represented. That is, the whole people of God. Thus, authority in the church is not rooted in the apostles and their descendants, but in the body itself. Therefore, pastoral authority is simply the exercise of oversight in the community of faith. This authority, Robinson rightly suggests, was "delegated by the rite of ordination, and thus the apostolic ministry was handed on from age to age within the church."[1] Robinson also reminds us that the church is

---

1   William Robinson, *The Biblical Doctrine of the Church*, Rev. Ed., (St. Louis: Bethany Press, 1955), p. 168.

neither a democracy, ruled by majority vote, nor is it an autocracy, the rule of an elite group of clergy. This is a difficult balance to maintain, yet it seems to be the biblical model.

If Jesus' ordination to ministry came at his baptism (Luke 3:21-22), then could we assume that baptism serves as a form of ordination for of God's people? If so, then all baptized Christians would be priests of God, with Jesus being the high priest. If this is true, then might we say that pastoral ministry is best defined as representative ministry. The pastor could be the bearer of a call to ministry that all Christians participate in. Standing in the pulpit or at the table, the pastor is not only a representative of God (as one who inspired by the Spirit speaks for God) but also as the representative of the people, sharing a message in word and sacrament that emerges from within the community itself.[1]

By thinking of pastoral ministry as representative ministry, we start with the premise that all ministry is important. No Christian is, by virtue of their office, holier than any other. There may be differences in roles and even *charism*, but not in importance to the health of the body. The calling of the pastoral leadership is not to do ministry for God's people but to equip and encourage the congregation in its ministries (Ephesians 4:11-13). In this it is helpful to note the difference in meaning that emerges when we compare the King James Version and the New Revised Standard when it comes to this passage. Note that in the King James verses 11 and 12 read:

> And he gave some, apostles; and some, prophets; and some, evangelists; and some, *pastors and teachers*; For the perfecting of the saints, *for the work of the ministry*, for the edifying of the body of Christ.

It appears here that these persons are given to the church to perfect the saints, do the work of the ministry and edify the body. But compare this with a modern rendering:

> The gifts he gave were that some would be apostles, some prophets, some evangelists, some pastors and teachers, to equip

---

1   Messer, *Images of Christian Ministry*, 64.

the saints for the work of ministry, for building up the body of Christ, . . .

In most modern translations, the purpose of the gifts of leadership is understood to be the equipping of the people of God for ministry not so they can do the ministry for them As Ephesians continues, we discover that the goal of pastoral ministry is to help God's people reach maturity in the Spirit, and that maturity leads to acts of service—the good works prepared for us by God.

When we look at ministry in this broader context our ordination to ministry comes at baptism, or as Kathleen Cahalan suggests, it is at the point at which we affirm our call to discipleship. Depending on your theology of baptism, these could be one and the same, but the point that Cahalan makes is that discipleship involves our responding to the call to follow Jesus, and that means "learning a way of life that embodies particular dispositions, attitudes, and practices that place the disciple in relationship to, and as a participant in, God's mission to serve and transform the world."[1] This description of ministry fits well with a missional calling—discipleship is an invitation to join with God in the missional work of serving and transforming the world.[2]

If we understand ordination to be an act of grace by which God uses the church to set persons apart for service to the world in Jesus Christ, whether through baptism or through the response to the call to discipleship, it is something that all Christians share in, then may we also affirm the principle that God might deem it wise for the church to set aside certain persons for specific forms of ministry, especially ministries of teaching and leadership? If so, then is it appropriate for the church to provide for public recogni-

1 Cahalan, *Introducing the Practice of Ministry*, p. 4.
2 Not everyone in the Christian community would affirm the premise that the church is called to engage in the ministry of transformation, at least in terms of the ministry of the church. John Nugent, for instance, suggests that efforts focused on fixing the world ultimately endanger the Gospel, thus he believes that the church should be the "better place" that stands as a beacon of what God has in store for the world. See Nugent, *Endangered Gospel, passim.*

tion of this calling? By recognizing persons whose gifts and calling leads toward a form of representative leadership that makes use of their spiritual gifts, the church is blessed by ministries of preaching, teaching, ministering the sacraments, administration, and pastoral care.

If God calls certain people to this kind of ministry, then surely there is some way of confirming this call. We hear people say all the time that God has called them to do this or that, but where is the confirmation? Does not the church have the responsibility to affirm this call and publicly confer on a person the authority to live into this office.[1] This seems to be the assumption of the author of 1 Timothy 4:14.

In ordaining a candidate for pastoral ministry, the church promises to hold the ordinand accountable to their calling. Although there are no double standards in Christian ministry, the church should expect that the ones upon whom they confer this title of pastor/clergy will hold themselves to the highest standards of behavior, that they will commit themselves to understanding this faith so that they may teach and equip others (making it imperative that those called to ordained ministry pursue some form of advanced education/training, if possible a traditional M.Div. program or an alternative program that covers the same competencies as the M.Div.).[2] Having had hands laid upon them, ordained pastors (my preferred title) stand as representatives of the church they serve. By extending the hands of ordination on candidates, the church declares to the broader church and the community at large, that this woman or man has been found to have the requisite gifts and calling to serve the church at large as pastors and teachers.

---

1   Watkins, *Great Thanksgiving,* p. 218.
2   A number of denominations have alternative forms of education. The Disciples of Christ, for instance, have set up an "apprentice track," that uses mentoring relationships under the jurisdiction of regions. The denomination has set out sixteen competencies that should mark the education of all clergy, no matter which track they enter . Other denominations have similar alternative pathways, which are often undertaken by second career clergy.

Although many clergy claim that they've felt God's leading or call to ministry, unless there is affirmation from the community how will one know if this is a true call or delusion? Is not the church charged with discerning both gifts and calling? This is an area in which faith communities struggle, for calling is personal, and yet those called will serve communities, and therefore communities have responsibility to help persons discern their call. For those charged with overseeing the process of moving from call, through preparation, to ordination, this can be a challenge. So, what role does ordination play in ministry, and what is our theology of ordination?

ACTION AND REFLECTION:

Find a copy of an ordination service. It could be your own or a recommended version of the denomination. What does this service say about the call to ministry? How does it lay out expectations for ministry? Does this service reflect the realities of ministry as you experience it?

Discussion:

1. What is the purpose and value of ordination?

2. How does a person discern a call to ordained ministry, and how does the faith community assist in this process?

3. In Christian circles, what role does baptism play in one's sense of call to ministry? Is there a difference between the baptism signified by baptism and the ordination signified by laying on of hands?

4. How does "ordained" ministry relate to "non-ordained" forms of ministry? Is there a hierarchical relationship implied in the call to ordained ministry?

5. How might faith communities hold clergy accountable to their ordination?

Epilogue:

Theology for Ministry in the Twenty-first Century

We live in a different world than our predecessors. Of course, the same could be said of them. Each generation of clergy faces a different set of challenges and opportunities. In the Chapter 6 of this book, we took a brief look at the potential and the pitfalls of ministry in the virtual world. While the forms it takes are different than might have previously been available, there are continuities. Most of us who are clergy engage with sacred texts that provide the touchstone. We may read them in different ways, but these texts are the starting point for our theological reflections. From there we touch base with the traditions passed on through the ages. They may or may not have the same level of authority as the primal texts, but they still speak with a degree of authority. I am influenced, even if I'm not aware of it, by those who have engaged in ministry down through the ages. I might acknowledge the influence of an Augustine, a Luther, a Barth, and a Moltmann, but my theology is also influenced by my engagement with the people with whom I studied and with whom I serve, whether ordained or lay.

Depending on your theology, the future may or may not be open. I happen to track with those who embrace an open future. That means that God may not know all the ins and outs of the future. Things could play out in a variety of ways. That means we have an important role to play in ministries that transform. It is important that we recognize that there may be differences between the faith we profess and the faith we practice. We serve among a people who believe, according to one study, in "a serviceable God." That is, "we want a God who meets our needs, who provides altars where we can get good service." Not only do we want a "serviceable God," but we want "a friendly God, who blesses us as we become comfortable, wealthy, and successful."[1]

This may be the world in which those called to ministry serve. Engaging in ministry that transforms lives might not fit such a cul-turally-relevant vision of religion. We may find it difficult to press on. We may be tempted to give up. I know I have! Having a strong theology of ministry, one that is deeply rooted in one's sacred texts and traditions, can provide a foundation for moving forward. The days ahead will be challenging, but that's the way it has always been. Clergy may not have the same cultural prominence as in earlier years. Congregations may struggle and decline in numbers, but as James Thompson suggests, ministry isn't really about numbers. It's about community formation and transformation. This is not to exclude ministry with individuals, but it is a recognition of the importance of community formation. Writing from a distinctively Christian perspective, Thompson writes that "The task of ministry is to create the climate in which congregations can be shaped by the cross and pursue the eschatological goal of transformation into the image of the Son."[2] My sense is that one can imagine a similar vision of ethical/community transformation emerging out of other faith traditions. The Hebrew Bible, for instance, is filled with such examples. Perhaps other traditions have similar resources that lead toward transformation and not simply cultural conformation.

Is there hope for the future? It is unlikely that the church will return to the halcyon days of yore, when the pews were full and the treasury flush with money. Yes, there will be large churches, but most congregations will be small. For those feeling the call to vocational ministry may find fewer opportunities to find gainful employment. Bivocational ministry might become more the norm than the exception. As we look at the "profession" we may decide it

---

1   Juan M. Floyd-Thomas, Stacey M. Floyd-Thomas, and Mark G. Toulouse, *The Altars Where We Worship: The Religious Significance of Popular Culture*, (Louisville: Westminster John Knox Press, 2016), pp. 1-2.

2   Thompson, *Pastoral Ministry According to Paul*, p. 162.

is not worth pursuing, especially considering the increasing cost of theological education. Nevertheless, the call to ministry still goes out. Women and men hear and respond. Ultimately the hunger for a word from God remains strong. Therefore, the mission of the church remains ever with us, but not as a duty to be fulfilled, but as an expression of joy in being a community called by God to be a blessing to the nations. Lesslie Newbigin writes that in the New Testament "Mission begins with a kind of explosion of joy. The news that the rejected and crucified Jesus is alive is something that cannot possibly be suppressed. It must be told." In fact, Newbigin, who is often seen as the founder of the modern missional movement, speaks of mission in terms of the "fallout of a vast explosion, radioactive fallout which is not lethal but life-giving."[1] In an age of change that leads to fear and anxiety, this is good news, and a calling worthy to be embraced. It's not an easy calling. One doesn't get rich doing it. Yet, it is a worthy calling. The question is, who will respond?

I close here with the call of Jeremiah. This prophet of the exile, faced a difficult task. His congregation lived in fear and anxiety. They were, after all, living in exile. But perhaps that image is an apt one, for in many ways we are called to serve communities of faith living in exile. So, we hear the call:

[4] The Lord's word came to me:

[5] "Before I created you in the womb I knew you;
　　before you were born I set you apart;
　　I made you a prophet to the nations."
[6] "Ah, Lord God," I said, "I don't know how to speak
　　because I'm only a child."
[7] The Lord responded,
　　"Don't say, 'I'm only a child.'
　　　Where I send you, you must go;
　　　what I tell you, you must say.

---

1 Lesslie Newbigin, *The Gospel in a Pluralist Society,* (Grand Rapids: Wm. B. Eerdmans Publishing Company, 1989), p. 116.

[8] Don't be afraid of them,
    because I'm with you to rescue you,"
        declares the Lord.
[9] Then the Lord stretched out his hand,
    touched my mouth, and said to me,
    "I'm putting my words in your mouth.
[10] This very day I appoint you over nations and empires,
    to dig up and pull down,
    to destroy and demolish,
    to build and plant." (Jeremiah 1:4-10 CEB).

BIBLIOGRAPHY

Baker, Kendall Clark. *When Faith Storms the Public Square: Mixing Religion and Politics through Community Organizing to Enhance our Democracy.* Cleveland: Circle Books, 2011.

Baptism, Eucharist, and Ministry Document; Faith and Order Paper number 111. http://www.oikoumene. org/en/resources/documents/wcc-commissions/ faith-and-order-commission/i-unity-the-church-and-its-mission/bap- tism-eucharist-and-ministry-faith-and-order-paper-no-111- the-lima-text/baptism-eucharist-and-ministry.html#c10500.

Barber II, William J. with Jonathan Wilson-Hartgrove. *The Third Reconstruction: Moral Mondays, Fusion Politics, and the Rise of a New Justice Movement.* Boston: Beacon Press, 2016.

Bass, Diana Butler. *Christianity After Religion: The End of Church and the Birth of a New Spiritual Awakening.* San Francisco: Harper One, 2012.

Beck, Richard. *Reviving Old Scratch: Demons and the Devil for Doubters and the Disenchanted.* Minneapolis: Fortress Press, 2016.

Bonhoeffer, Dietrich. *Life Together. Prayer Book of the Bible. (Dietrich Bonhoeffer Works, Volume 5).* English Edition edited by Geffrey B. Kelly. Translated by Daniel W. Bloesch and James H. Burtness. Minneapolis: Fortress Press, 1996.

Cahalan, Kathleen. *Introducing the Practice of Ministry.* Collegeville, MN: Liturgical Press, 2010.

Campbell, Alexander. *Compend of Alexander Campbell's Theology.* Edited by Royal Humbert. St. Louis: Bethany Press, 1961.

Clayton, Philip, with Tripp Fuller. *Transforming Christian Theology for Church and Society.* Minneapolis: Fortress Press, 2010.

Cornwall, Robert D. *Ephesians: A Participatory Bible Study.* Gonzalez, FL: Energion Publications, 2011.

_____. *Freedom in Covenant: Reflections on the Distinctive Values and Practices of the Christian Church (Disciples of Christ).* Eugene, OR: Wipf and Stock, 2015.

_____. *Unfettered Spirit: Spiritual Gifts for a New Great Awakening.* Gonzalez, FL: Energion Publications, 2013.

Disciplesnet Church. http://www.disciplesnet.org/about-us/misvis.

Epperly, Bruce. "Encouraging Lay Theology," *Alban at Duke Divinity School.* https://alban.org/2016/08/16/bruce-epperly-encouraging-lay-theology.

Epperly, Bruce G. and Katherine Gould Epperly. *Tending to the Holy: The Practice of the Presence of God in Ministry.* Herndon, VA: Alban Books, 2009.

Floyd-Thomas, Juan M., Stacey M. Floyd-Thomas, and Mark G. Toulouse. *The Altars Where We Worship: The Religious Significance of Popular Culture.* Louisville: Westminster John Knox Press, 2016.

Jones, Joe R. *A Lover's Quarrel: A Theologian and His Beloved Church.* Eugene, OR: Cascade Books, 2014.

_____. *On Being the Church of Jesus Christ in Tumultuous Times.* Eugene, OR: Cascade Books, 2005.

Jones, Tony. *The Church is Flat.* Minneapolis: JoPa Productions, 2011.

McFague, Sallie. *The Body of God: An Ecological Theology.* Minneapolis: Fortress Press, 1993.

Messer, Donald. *Contemporary Images of Christian Ministry.* Nashville: Abingdon Press, 1989.

Moltmann, Jürgen. *The Church in the Power of the Spirit: A Contribution to Messianic Ecclesiology*, Translated by Margaret Kohl. New York: Harper and Row, Publishers, 1977.

Newbigin, Lesslie. *The Gospel in a Pluralist Society.* Grand Rapids: Wm. B. Eerdmans Publishing Company, 1989.

Nugent, John C. *Endangered Gospel: How Fixing the World is Killing the Church.* Eugene, OR: Cascade Books, 2016.

Piatt, Christian and Amy Piatt, *MySpace to Sacred Space: God for a New Generation,* (St. Louis: Chalice Press, 2007.

Robinson, William. *The Biblical Doctrine of the Church.* Revised Edition. St. Louis: Bethany Press, 1955.

Salvatierra, Alexia and Peter Heltzel. *Faith-Rooted Organizing: Mobilizing the Church in Service to the World.* Downers Grove, IL: Intervarsity Press, 2014.

Sparks, Paul, Tim Soerens, and Dwight J. Friesen. *The New Parish: How Neighborhood Churches are Transforming Mission, Discipleship and Community.* Downers Grove: IVP Books, 2014.

Thompson, Deanna. *The Virtual Body of Christ in a Suffering World.* Nashville: Abingdon Press, 2016.

Thompson, James W. *Pastoral Ministry According to Paul.* Grand Rapids: Baker Academic, 2006.

Van Gelder, Craig. *The Ministry of the Missional Church: A Community Led by the Spirit.* Foreword by Alan J. Roxburgh. Grand Rapids: Baker Books, 2007.

Watkins, Keith. *Thankful Praise: A Resource for Christian Worship.* St. Louis: CBP Press, 1987.

_____. *The Great Thanksgiving.* St. Louis: Chalice Press, 1995.

Wesley, John. *Journal of John Wesley,* in the *Christian Classics Ethereal Library*—http://www.ccel.org/ccel/wesley/journal.vi.iii.v.html

Willimon, William H. "Introduction." *The Word in this World: Two Sermons by Karl Barth.* Edited by Kurt I. Johanson. Vancouver, BC: Regent College Publishing, 2007. Pages 10-22.

ALSO FROM ENERGION PUBLICATIONS
and the Academy of Parish Clergy

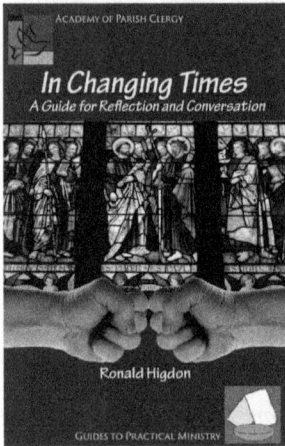

He is a modern-day prophet, savvy enough to know that the future is not as important as today yet that the future depends on what we do today.

Bo Prosser, Ed.D.
Coordinator of Organizational
Relationships
Cooperative Baptist Fellowship

ALSO BY BOB CORNWALL

Bob Cornwall here shows that the gifts of the Spirit are not owned by the pentecostal-charismatic wing of the church. Rather, the time is now for mainline churches to reappropriate the full spectrum of the spiritual gifts for their contemporary tasks.

Amos Young, Ph.D.

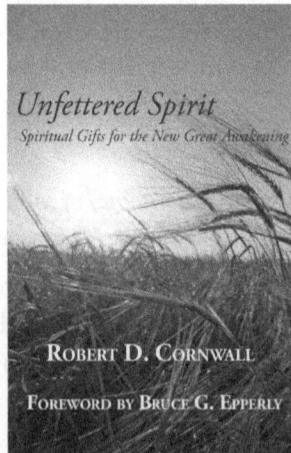

MORE FROM ENERGION PUBLICATIONS

Personal Study

Finding My Way in Christianity	Herold Weiss	$16.99
Holy Smoke! Unholy Fire	Bob McKibben	$14.99
The Jesus Paradigm	David Alan Black	$17.99
When People Speak for God	Henry Neufeld	$17.99
The Sacred Journey	Chris Surber	$11.99

Christian Living

Faith in the Public Square	Robert D. Cornwall	$16.99
Grief: Finding the Candle of Light	Jody Neufeld	$8.99
Crossing the Street	Robert LaRochelle	$16.99

Bible Study

Learning and Living Scripture	Lentz/Neufeld	$12.99
Inspiration: Hard Questions, Honest Answers	Alden Thompson	$39.99
Philippians: A Participatory Study Guide	Bruce Epperly	$9.99
Colossians: A Participatory Study Guide	Allan R. Bevere	$12.99
Ephesians: A Participatory Study Guide	Robert D. Cornwall	$9.99

Theology

Ultimate Allegiance	Robert D. Cornwall	$9.99
The Church Under the Cross	William Powell Tuck	$11.99
The Journey to the Undiscovered Country	William Powell Tuck	$9.99
Death, Immortality, and Resurrection	Edward W. H. Vick	$14.99
From Here to Eternity	Bruce Epperly	$5.99

Academy of Parish Clergy

Clergy Table Talk	Kent Ira Groff	$9.99
Wind and Whirlwind	David Moffett-Moore	$9.99
Overcoming Sermon Block	William Powell Tuck	$12.99
In Changing Times	Ron Higdon	$14.99
Thrive	Ruth Fletcher	$14.99

Generous Quantity Discounts Available
Dealer Inquiries Welcome
Energion Publications — P.O. Box 841
Gonzalez, FL_ 32560
Website: http://energionpubs.com
Phone: (850) 525-3916

www.ingramcontent.com/pod-product-compliance
Lightning Source LLC
Chambersburg PA
CBHW031603040426
42452CB00006B/393

9 781631 993732